PRAISE FOR
COACHING GIRLS' SOFTBALL

"New coaches, as well as all seasoned coaches of young girls playing softball, will want to have this book. Strahan gives insightful help for handling situations unique to coaching young girls."

—Margo Jonker, 2000 Assistant USA Olympic Softball Coach and Head Softball Coach, Central Michigan University

"This is a wonderful guide to enriching and enlightening the mind, body, and spirit of any coach, as well as of the athletes. Coach Strahan has done an outstanding job of detailing what it takes to be an effective and successful softball coach on any level. This is a must-have in any softball coach's library!"

—Rhonda Revelle, President, National Fastpitch Coaches Association (NFCA); Head Softball Coach, University of Nebraska

"*Coaching Girls' Softball,* written by one of the game's best players and coaches, is an excellent resource for every softball player and coach today. This valuable book covers many important and forgotten aspects of softball that players and coaches need to know."

—Kelly Jackson, All American Softball School Owner/Director, Junior Olympic Softball Commissioner, ASA All American and MVP, Redding Rebel 17-year veteran and National Champion

COACHING GIRLS' SOFTBALL

**From the How-To's of the Game to Practical
Real-World Advice—Your Definitive Guide
to Successfully Coaching Girls**

KATHY STRAHAN

Prima Publishing

Dedicated to Bill and Jean Strahan, my parents, for their love and support throughout my playing career and to this day still. Thank you for giving me the chance to play all the sports I could as a kid and for allowing me to be the athlete that I would become! I love you both.

Published by Prima Publishing, Roseville, California. Member of the Crown Publishing Group, a division of Random House, Inc.

PRIMA PUBLISHING and colophon are registered trademarks of Random House, Inc., registered with the United States Patent and Trademark Office.

Illustrations by Pamela Tanzey and Andrew Vallas

Library of Congress Cataloging-in-Publication Data
Strahan, Kathy.
    Coaching girls' softball : from the how-to's of the game to practical real-world advice, your definitive guide to successfully coaching girls / Kathy Strahan.
        p. cm.
    Includes index.
    ISBN 0-7615-3250-1
    1. Softball for women—Coaching.   I. Title.

GV881.3 .577 2001
796.357'8—dc21   2001033177

02 03 04 II 10 9 8 7 6 5 4 3 2
Printed in the United States of America

First Edition

Visit us online at www.primapublishing.com

CONTENTS

Acknowledgments   vii

Introduction   ix

CHAPTER 1   **So You Want to Be a Coach**   1
Role of the Coach   2
Time Commitment   4
Leadership   6
Coaching Style   9
Liability   12

CHAPTER 2   **Strategies for Coaching the Young Female Athlete**   19
Effective Communication   20
Effective Teaching   24
Team Discipline   29
Motivating Athletes   31
Being a Good Role Model   35

CHAPTER 3   **Coaching Girls**   39
How Girls and Boys Play Sports   40
Physical Differences Between Boys and Girls   42
Psychological Differences Between Boys and Girls   44
Serious Issues in Softball Today   46
Sexual Harassment   53

CHAPTER 4   **Softball Basics**   57
Equipment   58
Position Play   63
Choosing a Support Staff   70
The Game   72

CHAPTER 5   **The How-To's of Individual Defensive Play**   **81**
How to Throw   82
How to Catch   89
How to Field Ground Balls   93
How to Field Fly Balls   97
How to Pitch   100
How to Catch a Pitch   109

CHAPTER 6   **The How-To's of Individual Offensive Play**   **115**
How to Bat   116
How to Bunt   122
How to Run the Bases   132
How to Slide   142

CHAPTER 7   **Offensive Strategies in Team Play**   **143**
How to Use Offensive Team Strategies   143
How to Communicate Through Signs and Signals   147

CHAPTER 8   **Defensive Strategies in Team Play**   **151**
How to Execute Basic Defensive Situations   152
How to Run the Transition Game   154
How to Execute the Bunt Defense   158
How to Execute the Double Play   162
How to Execute the Rundown   165
How to Execute the First and Third Play   168

CHAPTER 9   **Planning for the Season**   **171**
How to Set Goals   172
How to Conduct a Parent Meeting   176
How to Plan Practice   177
How to Condition Your Team   181
How to Prepare for Game Day   182

CHAPTER 10   **Conclusion**   **187**

Appendix: Organizations   **191**

Glossary   **193**

References   **197**

Index   **199**

About the Author   **209**

ACKNOWLEDGMENTS

I WISH TO ACKNOWLEDGE the following people who made this book possible in one way or another.

To my brother Jim—thanks for never missing a game and for being my biggest fan. And to my brother Jeff—I am very proud of you for the man you've become. I love both of you guys.

Thank you Tami, Taz, Bailey, and Karly for your patience and understanding of the time it took me to put this book together. Your love means everything.

I have two great assistant coaches in Debbie Bilbao and Jennifer Fritz. Thanks for picking up the slack with the team when it was time to work on this book. I couldn't have done it without you.

Thank you Kay Purves, my first softball coach, for your tutelage and for seeing my potential. And to Ralph Raymond, who coached me at the end of my playing career—thank you for giving me the greatest opportunity of my life; a playing opportunity with the best softball team ever, the Raybestos Brakettes.

INTRODUCTION

WHEN I WAS FIVE years old, I could swing a bat as well as any major league baseball player. At least, that's what my father told me. We'd spend hours in the backyard playing catch, then he'd pitch whiffle balls to me until the sun went down. As I grew older, my mother stepped in with the "playing catch" routine. My career as a softball player was beginning to take off, and I wanted to improve. It took practice, but I loved it, and my parents were always there to help out.

In those early days, there weren't many girls' teams, and youth sports involved kids playing ball at the park down the street. I was on a softball team in the local recreation league with other girls my age. We had a female coach, organized practices, and played games a few nights a week. An older, red-haired girl played first base on my team, and she always complained that I threw the ball too hard. That's when I started to realize I might be a little ahead of my time in skill development. How can a 12-year-old throw the ball too hard from shortstop?

When it was time to go to high school, a new school had just been built in my district. That first year only sophomores and juniors were in attendance. The girls' softball team was organized that year, and their jerseys consisted of bright orange shirts with big black numbers on the back. Cut-off blue jean shorts served as bottoms to complete the uniform ensemble. The team wasn't very good, and I didn't want to play with them.

The boys on the baseball team, however, looked like ballplayers. They had white uniforms with black pinstripes, orange stirrup socks, and white baseball caps with orange bills. Now that was a uniform! It was obvious that my skills far exceeded the level of play on the girls' team, and I wanted to compete with other skilled athletes. I tried out for boys' baseball and made the team. Trying out and getting through the conditioning was extremely challenging. I almost fainted during one long-distance run, but I persevered. And the best part? The first baseman didn't complain that I threw the ball too hard from shortstop!

I don't know if I was the first girl to play high school baseball, but being the only girl on a boys' team in Lansing, Michigan, in 1973 created a little controversy. The early seventies were a time of dramatic change for women in sport, not only in Lansing, Michigan, but throughout the country as well. Women athletes were beginning to cry out for equal opportunities in sports, and if the teams weren't there, then women were going to compete with the men. And so the battle of the sexes began.

LEVELING THE PLAYING FIELD

In 1972, Congress passed Title IX of the Educational Amendment Act. This was a ban on sex discrimination in all educational programs receiving federal assistance. It was supposed to open the door for girls and women in sports and "level the playing field." Although Title IX eventually helped my high school softball team get uniforms comparable to those of the baseball team, there were many improvements left to be made. Inequitable sport budgets, playing fields, schedules, and coaching staffs—both in the number of coaches available to boys' and girls' teams and coaches' qualifications—became Title IX issues. In nearly every category in every sport, girls' sports participation wasn't taken seriously.

With the passage of Title IX, increasing numbers of girls and women began to enter the athletic arena to compete. The Women's Sports Foundation reported in 1999 that girls who participate in sports have higher self-esteem than those who do not, and that participation in physical activity reduces symptoms of stress and depression. As teenagers, girls who participate in sports are less than half as likely to get pregnant as those girls who do not participate.

Girls learn social skills, teamwork, responsibility, discipline, and build self-esteem through play. Sports are a way for girls to feel connected with one another, sharing experiences in learning about themselves and others, which is a valuable part of the growth and maturation process. Finding success in failure, and discovering that failure is an opportunity for growth, was a valuable part of growing up for me. Hard work, perseverance, and giving my best effort on the field of play prepared me for a lifetime of success.

As more women entered the athletic arena, sports organizations began to swell with participation numbers. The Amateur Softball Association (ASA) reports that the number of registered girls' Junior Olympic (18 and under—all divisions) fast-pitch softball teams grew from 46,119 in 1994 to just over 65,900 in 1999.

The National Collegiate Athletic Association (NCAA) has also seen a steady increase in collegiate institutions sponsoring softball. In 1984, 451 NCAA member institutions sponsored the sport of softball. Today, 860 sponsor the sport. The NCAA reported in 1998 that one of the primary reasons for the increase is Title IX. Softball is a viable women's sport to add to institutions that want to balance spending between men's and women's programs for Title IX compliance.

Fast-pitch softball reached celebrity status when Team USA won the gold medal in the 1996 Olympic Games. Team members Lisa Fernandez and Dr. Dot Richardson became household names almost overnight. These two gold medalists captivated the hearts of thousands of young girls, who signed up for softball teams in droves to play just like their new Olympic heroes. A 1999–2000 High School Athletics Participation Survey, conducted by The National Federation of State High School Associations (NFSHSA), reports that fast-pitch softball ranks fourth behind basketball, track/field, and volleyball, in a list of the ten most popular girls' high school sports. In a top ten ranking of the numbers of girls participating in high school sports, fast-pitch softball also ranks fourth, with 343,001 participants. And Team USA's repeat performance of winning gold in the 2000 Olympic Games is unlikely to slow the influx of young girls into the sport of softball.

WHY KIDS PLAY SPORTS

Research has shown that one of the primary reasons kids play sports is to have fun. When playing ceases to be enjoyable, kids quit, and if their experience is especially negative, they tend to shy away from sports altogether. One of the great things about softball is that just about anyone can play it. A child doesn't have to possess a certain body type to experience success and to have fun. In gymnastics, for example, girls with smaller, petite body types are more likely to experience success in executing movements on the beam, in vaulting, on the parallel bars, or in floor exercise routines than girls with larger, heavier builds. Softball players come in all different shapes and sizes. Kids don't have to be thin, tall, fast, or strong, nor do they have to possess any other such characteristics to be successful and have fun. All they need is the desire to play.

As more girls choose to play softball, there will be a need for more teams and more coaches to coach those teams. Expectations of youth sport coaches entering the coaching arena are taking a new direction. Coaches are expected to provide a positive experience for kids, control angry parents and spectators, and be accountable for all aspects of the sport program. National organizations for youth sports are calling for certification of youth coaches. Coaches can have a tremendous influence on young people and that impact can last a lifetime. It is no longer suitable to have a youth sports coach whose background consists of having played a little baseball or softball in high school.

WHY THIS BOOK?

Every year I receive phone calls from coaches who have just taken on a girls' softball team and don't quite know where to start. Frequently, a call comes from a father who has just signed up his daughter for Bobby Sox softball, and the team needs a coach. Because he played a little baseball in high school, he is one of the more "qualified" parents on the team, so he volunteers to coach the team. He knows that although softball and baseball are very similar games, there are some differences as well. He asks if I have any information available to help get him started. And then there's the matter of coaching girls. Is it the same as coaching boys? My answer is sometimes yes, and sometimes no.

There are a number of books on the subject of coaching girls' softball. Most are filled with how to execute the basic skills with drills and sport strategies. But there's not much information for an entry-level coach who is taking on a whole new sports entity. Should girls be coached the same as boys? Are their attitudes, behaviors, and the reasons they play the same as boys? How does a coach deal with parents today? Should there be team rules? How long should practice be? And what about serious issues like sexual harassment and eating disorders? Feeling overwhelmed? Then this book might be for you.

This book is for coaches of girls ages 7 to 13. It is a culmination of my total involvement in softball, from my educational experience, to my experiences as a player and a coach. It encompasses the latest research, as well as discussions and interviews with other coaches in the field.

After high school, I attended and graduated from Michigan State University (MSU) with an undergraduate degree in kinesiology. I remained at MSU and received my master's degree in motor development with a cognate in sports psychology. While in college, I played softball and basketball and helped guide MSU to the AIAW National Softball Championship in 1976. On the amateur level, I played short-stop for the Raybestos Brakettes and was a part of three national championship teams. I was also a member of the United States team that won the World Championship in 1978 and went on to compete for the United States and win a gold medal in the Pan American Games in 1979. At the end of my playing career, coaching opportunities presented themselves, so I decided to become a coach.

Throughout my coaching career, I have worked with girls and young women. Early in my career, I coached high school girls and then migrated into the college ranks where I am today. I have spent 20 years at the collegiate level, mostly as a head coach at the NCAA Division I level. I have worked with hundreds of young women, and experienced the ups and downs of games, seasons, careers, and lives as we have lived them.

If you're a beginning coach, and want to use this book as a starting point, it will help you find the way. Softball techniques are presented in a straightforward manner with drills and coaching tips provided where appropriate. If you feel confident in your general knowledge of the game and want some insight into working with female athletes, this book will shed some light on how and why they play, and will give you suggestions to use as a coach. This book also addresses serious issues you must be aware of on a day-to-day basis. Sexual harassment, the stresses of competition, and obsession with weight and eating disorders are part of a growing body of knowledge that coaches are expected to have prior to entering the coaching domain today.

Use this book as you see fit. Provide a positive learning environment for your athletes, keep open lines of communication, teach to the best of your ability, and be sensitive to your athletes' needs. Accept responsibility for the program and make sure your expectations are clearly understood by everyone involved. Take time to listen to those around you and always try to make fair and consistent decisions. You have a tremendous impact on the lives you touch as a coach, and your role should never be taken lightly. Keep abreast of new information and attend coaching clinics often. Coaching can be a very powerful and rewarding experience. And maybe you'll find, like I have, that it is always a special moment each and every time I hear an athlete call me "coach."

1

So You Want to Be a Coach

It's your first day of practice with your new team and 16 girls are sitting on the ground looking up at you. You are their coach, and they wait for your direction. Some girls are excited, others are a little nervous, and a few are talking to their friends. Some have new gloves and new shoes, and others look like seasoned professionals. There they are, with their parents watching from nearby. You want to get off to a great start and make this a positive experience for everyone involved. But before you reach your first practice, you need to understand what is involved in coaching.

Simply put, coaching is teaching. Coaching is, however, much more than teaching your athletes the skills and strategies of the game. At times, you will be expected to serve as a teacher, parent, counselor, sport psychologist, medic, or mediator. You will also be expected to enforce law and order to a certain extent. You will not only develop the physical skills of your young softball players, but you will also influence their personal, psychological, and social development.

Coaching involves a lot of your time, both on and off the field, and the commitment you make is a serious one—a commitment that you and your family must be willing to make together. You will need

1

strong leadership skills to provide the direction that others will follow. You will need to formulate your coaching style and effectively run your program. It is incumbent upon you to ensure your athletes' safety and to protect yourself from liability. If you take the time to be organized, to plan effectively, to communicate clearly, and to understand what coaching entails, then you will likely have a rewarding experience coaching softball.

ROLE OF THE COACH

Your role as coach is simple, but the responsibilities can be enormous. Your basic role is to provide a positive experience for the athletes playing on your team. You can't be all things to all people, and you can't ensure that everything will always turn out right. You will, however, be responsible for the overall running of the program and will be held accountable should something go wrong. You are the coach, and it is up to you to provide the leadership and direction that is beneficial to the members of your team.

Coaching Tip

Attend coaches' clinics. Watch the top women's softball in your area. Expand your knowledge to broaden your understanding of the game, give you new ideas for drills and techniques, and keep you abreast of trends.

A coach is in a position of authority. You have tremendous influence on your young athletes, and that should not be taken lightly. The things you say, the way you act and approach situations, will likely leave a lasting impression on the kids. Be a good role model and do everything you reasonably can to protect and care for them. Learn as much as you can about softball and coaching effectively. Attend coach's clinics and watch top-notch women's softball in your area to become more knowledgeable and keep up to date on the game. Be positive and provide your athletes with a fun learning environment to help shape their personal, social, and psychological development.

To ensure a positive experience for your athletes, you must focus on the things you can control. You can't control the parents, umpires, weather, or how your athletes will respond to certain situations, but you can control how you act, how you teach, the things you say, and how you prepare yourself and your team. Be aware of what you do and how it effects your athletes. Focus on the things you, as a coach, can control (see table 1.1) and be aware of how children are likely to be affected by them.

Table 1.1 Positive and negative coaching techniques and their likely impact on a young athlete	
Positive Coaching Techniques	**Likely Affect on Child**
1. Teaches proper skills/mechanics	1. Experiences success; builds self-esteem
2. Properly conditions athletes	2. Experiences improvement in performance; less likely to be injured
3. Structures drills/progressions for success	3. Experiences improvement in performance, which builds self-confidence
4. Keeps learning fun, uses different drills	4. Enjoys activity; stays involved longer
5. Demands respect for rules and fair play	5. Learns respect for authority; values sportsmanship
6. Develops positive interpersonal skills	6. Builds self-worth, self-esteem, self-control; learns value of teamwork
7. Is cognizant of athlete's safety/welfare	7. Builds trust and respect for coach
Negative Coaching Techniques	**Likely Affect on Child**
1. Teaches improper mechanics/skills	1. Fails; lowers self-esteem; increased risk of injury
2. Poorly conditions athletes	2. Performance suffers; more likely to be injured
3. Drills too hard; no progression	3. Fails to improve; lowers self-confidence
4. Doesn't make activity fun	4. Loses interest; drops out of softball
5. Breaks rules, poor sportsmanship	5. Learns to disrespect authority; antisocial behavior
6. Always criticizes athletes	6. Hates softball; can't do anything right; quits team
7. Ignores athlete's safety/welfare	7. Loss of trust and respect for coach

DIRT FROM THE DIAMOND

Phil Soto coaches the 10-and-under California Breeze, an Amateur Softball Association (ASA) team in Sacramento, California. He says the time commitment for him is daily. In addition to games and practices, Phil attends fund-raisers and conducts developmental clinics. Although a handful of games are played in the fall, the traditional season for Phil begins in February and runs through August. The Breeze 10-and-under team plays between 80 and 90 games in a typical year (about 25 games in the fall and the rest during the summer season). During the summer, the team travels nearly every single weekend. According to Phil, "We'll practice twice a week during the summer. We usually start at 6:00 P.M. and end when the sun goes down. But," he adds, "the kids bring the energy with them. I'll be tired at the end of practice, but they'll ask me to hit more ground balls, and they just keep you going."

Phil has a wife and three kids. He coaches his daughter on the team as well, so traveling with the team has become a family affair. Phil has been coaching for years, and his family understands the commitment. Although he has a full-time job elsewhere, he loves coaching his team. He does it, he says, because he has fun.

TIME COMMITMENT

Coaching a girl's softball team is time-consuming. It involves more than showing up for games and practices. Take the time to methodically plot out the season and plan for the level of commitment that will be required of you.

Although this time commitment will involve you as the coach, it will also affect your family. There will be games, practices, meetings with athletes and parents, perhaps travel, and various other activities, depending upon the competitive level of your team or organization. Some teams travel quite frequently, and because of the additional costs involved with travel, those organizations often require additional time commitments from players, parents, and coaches to conduct fund-raisers, such as car washes and bingo.

To determine the amount of time you'll be required to commit, make a calendar of all the games and practice dates. Will you be required to attend board or league meetings? If so, include those dates on the calendar. Will you be required to raise funds for team travel or equipment? If so, what kinds of activities will you do and when will you do them? Mark those dates on your calendar as well. Be sure to schedule a parent meeting on your calendar. Will you want to have more than one meeting? If there will be tryouts for your team, how much time will that take? Have you thought about social activities, such as get-togethers for your kids to make being on the team fun?

Once you have a calendar put together, discuss the time commitment with your family. There may be times when your family can travel with you or be involved in the various activities you have planned.

In addition to your own time commitment, it is important that players and their parents understand the commitment required on their part. Save yourself some headaches and be clear about how much time is expected from players and parents in the very beginning. When you conduct tryouts for your team, or when you first meet with parents and athletes, discuss the dedication involved. You don't want kids to quit because they didn't understand the expectations.

TIME COMMITMENT CALENDAR CHECKLIST

Make a calendar with the dates, times, and locations of the following events and activities. Check off each item on the list once you include all dates for that activity on your calendar.

❑ Tryout dates, times, and locations

❑ Dates of games, times, and locations

❑ Practice times and locations

❑ Dates of board/league meeting times and locations

❑ Date(s) of parent meeting(s), times, and locations

❑ Dates of fund-raisers, times, and locations

❑ Dates of team social activities, times, and locations

❑ Other (list)

DIRT FROM THE DIAMOND

When I played shortstop for the Raybestos Brakettes in Stratford, Connecticut, I was fortunate to have Ralph Raymond as a coach. The Brakettes were, and still are, a women's ASA major team and have one of the most successful histories of winning in all of sport. So much so, that the Raybestos Brakettes have been profiled in a book about some of the greatest teams of all time, along with the likes of the New York Yankees, the Dallas Cowboys, and the Boston Celtics. Ralph was the coach behind the Brakette dynasty of the sixties and seventies, and he continues to be successful today. As the head coach of the U.S. Olympic softball team, he led the squads to gold medals in both the Atlanta, 1996, and Sydney, 2000, Olympic Games.

Ralph Raymond has been one of the most influential people in my life. He had a hand in shaping much of how I am and what I do as a coach. He always told us that there could only be one chief, and the rest had to be Indians. For the team to be successful, there could only be one leader, the coach. Everyone else had to follow directions. Otherwise, you would have a bunch of assistant coaches and players working independently of one another, the common goal of the team—to be successful— would never be achieved.

LEADERSHIP

Understanding essential leadership skills is the next step. You will be looked upon to provide the leadership and direction, which parents, athletes, and your own coaching staff will follow.

Clearly the ability to be a good coach or leader is more than simply giving directions for athletes to follow. Ralph was much more than that. He had outstanding leadership ability. He had qualities as a coach that made us respect him, believe in him, and trust that in following his direction, we would be successful as a team.

The first quality of leadership is that you must want to lead! You must have the drive, courage, and capability to be in charge. According to Wess Roberts, in *Leadership Secrets of Attila the Hun*, you must also be decisive, possess emo-

Coaching Tip

Be DECISIVE! When you vacillate or procrastinate, you cause confusion and discouragement.

tional stamina, and be self-confident. You must be committed to your cause and have a human quality about you that allows your players to know you care. Surely you will face obstacles, such as an overbearing parent, who thinks that his or her daughter is the best athlete on your team and should play shortstop rather than right field, but you must have the courage to act with confidence and accept the risks inherent in leadership.

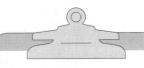

Coaching Tip

As a coach you are in a powerful position. Handle that power with care and don't abuse it. One of the best qualities of a powerful person is in never having to use the power!

Be decisive. You must know when to take action and when not to take action. The tendency towards vacillation and procrastination causes confusion and can lead to discouragement. I have a rule on my college team that if a player doesn't slide on a close play and is thrown out as a result of not sliding, she will be pulled from the game and replaced with a substitute. The reason for this rule is that I carry 20 athletes on my team, and I want them all to play hard and give 100 percent. Not sliding is lazy. Fortunately, this doesn't happen often, because my players learn to respect the rules and to trust that I will be fair in enforcing them.

On the other hand, it is sometimes best not to take any action at all. This is often the case when I see other team members move in to talk to a teammate about a particular action. When a player throws her batting helmet out of frustration after her turn "at-bat," teammates can often times be helpful in giving the player encouragement but warning her about the danger of throwing equipment. Peer pressure can be a powerful thing, and I'll monitor the situation from a distance. If it happens a second time, I will likely intervene.

Emotional stamina is an essential element of strong leadership ability. Leadership places increasing demands on the emotions of coaches. In sport, success is not a constant. Therefore, it is important to have the ability to bounce back quickly from disappointment, to see the positives in setbacks, and to keep a clear perspective. Losing perspective, or forgetting why you are coaching young athletes, can result in a negative environment. You should never be physical with an athlete or use threatening language toward players, officials, or spectators. If you feel yourself starting to lose perspective, talk with other coaches, take a short vacation, or start taking long walks. Think about what matters most to you in life. Remember, this is just a game.

To lead your team effectively, you must have self-confidence. Knowledge of the game, proper training in teaching and communication techniques, and self-preparedness give a new coach the self-assurance necessary to gain confidence and experience. Those who lack self-confidence will show signs of weakness to their athletes and assistant coaches, and will be viewed as weak leaders. This weakness often invites others to challenge authority, which usually results in conflict and a struggle for control.

DIRT FROM THE DIAMOND

When I was on the United States Pan American softball team in 1979, the games were in San Juan, Puerto Rico. Bobby Knight, the former basketball coach at Indiana University, was the head coach of the United States men's basketball team, also competing in the Pan Am Games at that same time. While we were in San Juan, there was an incident between Bobby Knight and a Puerto Rican police officer. Knight had allegedly hit the police officer, and many Puerto Ricans were outraged. For several days the mood of the people was very anti-U.S., and I was careful not to wear any clothing with the letters "U.S.A." emblazoned on it. Had Knight lost his temper and lashed out at somebody once again?

This incident reflected a temperament that was part of Coach Knight's personality as an individual. And this temperament was evident in how he was as a coach. He had a very controversial style of coaching then, and it apparently continued up until he was fired by Indiana University when he violated the university's "no tolerance" policy. It seems that not everyone was fond of Knight's coaching style.

TRAITS OF POSITIVE COACHING STYLE

- Possesses strong knowledge of the sport
- Listens to athletes and is empathetic
- Is a good role model
- Is fair and consistent in treatment of athletes
- Communicates clearly
- Lets athletes have input into some of the decision-making process
- Is motivational, positive, and encouraging
- Keeps softball fun
- Cares about athletes' personal and social development

COACHING STYLE

You have your own unique coaching style. How you react to an umpire who makes a bad call, what you say to your team after a heartbreaking loss, and how you treat your athletes are all reflective of your coaching style. Are you a positive coach, or are you negative? Do you lose your temper more than you should, and does it cause you to say things you wish you hadn't? Can you accept the fact that your athletes will disappoint you from time to time, and how will you handle it? You should be aware of how your style affects those around you.

Research in youth sports indicates that kids favor certain traits and characteristics in coaches. According to *Coaching Young Athletes*, kids like coaches who are knowledgeable about the sport and instructive, supportive and encouraging, understanding and reliable, and motivated and enthusiastic. They dislike coaches who are manipulative, indifferent, inconsistent, judgmental, or constantly negative.

Your role as a coach is to make sure the positives outweigh the negatives for any child who participates on your team. But, being a positive coach who responds to the needs of young athletes takes

Coaching Tip

Give praise to each individual team member during a practice.

discipline. If you keep in mind the positive coaching techniques and their likely effect on children, discussed earlier in this chapter, you will be well on your way to developing an effective coaching style.

What kind of a coach do you want to be? How will your personality fit into the kind of coach you become? Carefully consider how you will be viewed and what traits are likely to enable you to be successful. Some major league and college coaches may have success by using negative reinforcement and scare tactics, but your athletes aren't on scholarship, they aren't making millions of dollars, and their parents are unlikely to put up with an aggressive coaching style.

As a coach, you are shaping the attitudes, behaviors, beliefs, and perceptions of highly impressionable children who have connected to you through a mutual love for the sport of softball. Take time to listen to your athletes. Involve them in some of the decision-making process. Knowing you value their input will let them know that they are important and that you care about what they think. Be fair and consistent in your treatment of them. Accept the fact that your athletes will occasionally disappoint you, and use these opportunities to teach them about life. Lessons learned in sport have tremendous carry-over value later in life.

There are a number of coaching styles in sport today, and developing an effective coaching style is key to having a successful and rewarding experience in coaching. Be aware of positive coaching style traits and incorporate them into who you are as a coach. Make the sport enjoyable for the kids, and it will be enjoyable for you too!

Keys to Successful Coaching

If you follow the suggestions outlined in this book, you will win some games. But successful coaching isn't necessarily about winning. Success in coaching means achieving a favorable outcome. It can be about executing a play correctly that the team has been working on for weeks. Or, it can be about seeing the joy on the face of a 10-year-old after catching her first fly ball in a game and knowing that she had a positive experience.

Successful coaching is about teaching young athletes new skills, seeing them improve, allowing them to make friends and build relationships, and providing them with a positive experience overall. There are some keys to successful coaching that can't be overemphasized. As you read through the following list, honestly evaluate yourself and ask, Am I doing a good job? Here's what you should know.

1. ENTHUSIASM. Are you excited about coaching your team? Enthusiasm is contagious, and the more exuberance you show for what you are doing, the more the kids will feel your energy. Stay positive and show enthusiasm in your teaching and in your interaction with players and other coaches. Make practice activities fun. Let athletes know you enjoy what you're doing.

2. HONESTY. "Honesty is the best policy." It's an old cliché, but it certainly applies to coaching. Be honest with your players, coaches, and parents. When the message you have to deliver is a difficult one, be gentle, but be honest. Honesty gives you credibility, in that you know what you're doing and you have the information or expertise to back it up. People appreciate honesty, and by being honest, you set a great example for children to follow.

3. CONSISTENCY. Coaches are sometimes accused of playing favorites. Inconsistent treatment of athletes is one of the quickest ways to demoralize a team, and an athlete. Athletes expect fair treatment, be it playing time or rules enforcement. Consistency in the treatment of athletes builds trust and respect.

4. INTEGRITY. Integrity in coaching means, "do the right thing." Be the best you can be as a person and a coach. Model the kind of behavior you expect from your athletes and

Coaching Tip

Kids love to be part of decision making. Ask for suggestions about uniforms or where to eat after a game. They won't all agree. Take the top two choices and vote. Next time, go with the team's second pick.

assistant coaches. Respect officials, opponents, and the rules of the game. You will be teaching your players to do likewise.

5. ORGANIZATION. Have a plan for everything. Take time to plan for practices so kids aren't just standing around. Plan for the season, set goals, and determine activities and events. Organization eliminates chaos and confusion.

6. EMPATHY. Have an appreciation for, and an understanding of, the values of others. Take time to listen to kids and their parents. If you can, incorporate some of their feedback and ideas into your program. There may be a good idea out there that may make your program better. Put yourself in your athletes' position, and be sensitive to how they feel. Showing them you care can be the single most important thing you do for a young person.

LIABILITY

According to Rainer Martens in *Successful Coaching*, one of the scariest and most confusing parts of coaching has to do with liability. There are certain risks inherent in sports participation; however, if an injury is the result of improper supervision, teaching a skill incorrectly, or the failure on your part as a coach to reasonably ensure the safety of the equipment or the field of play, then you may be liable. In fulfilling your legal duties as a coach, it is your responsibility to conduct the sport of softball in a manner that is considered safe for your athletes and others. When you take every reasonable precaution to meet this legal duty, then you are managing risk.

Your Responsibility as a Coach

Our society is increasingly turning to the courts, sometimes for frivolous matters. If you fail, however, to fulfill your legal duty, then you may be considered negligent, and the courts are not likely to think of negligence as a frivolous matter. Think of your athletes as children first, and athletes second. Do everything you can to reasonably protect and care for them. Be more concerned with the learning process than with winning, and you will have gone a long way to help protect yourself from liability.

Check with your league on liability issues and insurance. Find out what your responsibilities are, whether or not you are insured, and what you should do if an injury occurs. Policies and procedures may already be in place and you can save yourself considerable angst by finding out in advance.

Creating a Safe Environment

One way to avoid injuries or other problems is to create a safe environment for your athletes. Know how to teach the skills of softball correctly. Be aware of progressions within the skills. For example, if an 8-year-old has difficulty catching a ball thrown from 30 feet, you wouldn't want to put her in the outfield and hit high fly balls to her. Instead, you might have her wear a catcher's mask while you gently toss softee balls in the air to help her improve her catching ability and keep her from being injured in the process.

Coaching Tip

Remember to walk the field and inspect it for holes, broken glass, and so forth prior to each practice and game. Make sure the bases are seated properly.

Make sure team equipment is safety-approved for your age group and is working correctly. Teach your athletes how to inspect the equipment as well. Tell them what to look for and to let you know of any irregularities. Catcher's masks, chest protectors, leg guards, and batting helmets are designed to protect the athletes if worn correctly. Explain to everyone on your team how to use the equipment properly, and what may happen if they don't. Check to see that the equipment fits the athlete and insist that it is worn whenever she is involved in that particular activity.

Because girls are of varying sizes and shapes, be attentive to how they are matched up in practices and games. Although you may have two 11-year-olds on the team, one may have the body of a 13-year-old biologically. If it is apparent that the latter is physically stronger to a significant degree, then you will want to separate them in specific throwing and catching drills to avoid injury.

Take time before games and practice to make sure the field is safe for play. Walk the grounds and look for broken glass, large rocks, holes that might cause an ankle injury, or a broken or protruding fence. If you use screens and pitching machines for practice, the screens should be secure and free of holes, and younger athletes should stay away from the machines and any electric cords.

Finally, make sure your team warms up properly. This will help prevent injuries. In the worst case, be prepared and have a plan in place for treating injuries.

Injury Prevention and Treatment

One way to prevent injuries is to prepare your athletes before games and practices. The proper sequence of events for a softball game or practice should consist of a warm-up (stretch routine, sprints, drills), main activity (game or practice), and cooldown (light stretching). Be sure to have a standard routine that the athletes automatically follow before and after physical activity.

The warm-up should start with easy jogging around the field for about five minutes. Athletes should then form a circle and follow a predetermined series of stretches and movements designed to loosen muscles and joints. Have one player lead the routine and sit in the middle of the circle. Rotate the responsibility of leading the stretching routine from practice to practice.

The stretching routine should take about ten minutes and should focus on all the major muscle groups. Specific stretches should be performed for the quadriceps, hamstrings, calves, hip flexors, inner thigh muscles, pecs (chest), biceps, and triceps. The stretches should be held for a 12 count. Never bounce when stretching. Instead, hold a steady position with the muscle on "stretch" for a 12 count and slowly lean into the stretch as you feel the muscle lengthen. Arm circles and trunk circles should also be included to help loosen the body.

Following the stretching routine, the athletes should run some sprints. Sprints should begin at about 50 percent of full speed on the

FIRST-AID KIT CONTENTS

❏ Emergency medical information on each athlete

❏ Emergency phone numbers and procedures

❏ Self-adhesive bandages

❏ Ice (quick ice packs)

❏ Gauze

❏ Sterile no-stick pads for cuts and abrasions

❏ Athletic tape

❏ Scissors

❏ Antiseptic wipes

❏ Wrapped sanitary feminine napkin

❏ Elastic wrap

❏ Tweezers

❏ Liquid soap

first one and gradually increase to 100 percent by the fourth or fifth sprint. Although you may want to use additional sprints for conditioning, some research cautions against high-level conditioning for this age group. According to Paul Vogel, in *Planning for the Season*:

> Generally, your primary concern for athletes in the 6–13 age range should be to develop physical skills, knowledge, and appropriate personal/social skills. This is not to suggest that conditioning is unimportant. It is, however, the studied opinion of many coaches and specialists in growth and development that the specific training designed to promote high levels of sport-related fitness should receive a lower priority at this age. . . . Part of the reason for this recommendation is that when young athletes train for skilled performance, they also obtain conditioning stimuli that are sufficient to cause the body to adapt to the fitness demands associated with learning and performing softball skills.

COMMON INJURIES AND PROPER FIRST AID

Bump, Bruise, or Sprain: Clean the area with soap and water, dry thoroughly and apply ice for 15 minutes. Keep athlete out of activity, resting.

Abrasion or Cut: Clean the area thoroughly with soap and water. Use an antiseptic wipe to sterilize the area. Elevate to control the bleeding if necessary. Apply a self-adhesive bandage or sterile no-stick pad and wrap with an elastic bandage.

Nose Bleed: Assist the athlete to a sitting position and have her pinch the nostrils together with her fingers while breathing through the mouth. Continue pinching nostrils until bleeding stops or call for medical assistance if bleeding is uncontrollable.

Cooldown activities similar to the warm-up activities should be incorporated following the main physical activity. Cooldowns include light jogging, stretching, and light activities specific to the sport, such as light throwing. The cooldown routine should take approximately five minutes.

Even with proper warm-ups and cooldowns, accidents still happen. Therefore, stock a first-aid kit with the basics, and keep

COACHING LIABILITY CHECKLIST

Check off each item as you complete the task.

❑ Check league policy for insurance and liability information.

❑ Establish procedures for handling an injury on the team (keep in first-aid kit).

❑ Keep a record of medical information obtained on all players (keep in first-aid kit).

❑ Keep first-aid kit stocked and on-site for all games and practices.

❑ Ensure that coaches/staff are trained and knowledgeable of procedures and liability issues.

❑ Inspect softball equipment for safety and show athletes proper use.

it at every practice and game. You should have all emergency medical information on each athlete, and signed waivers from parents if required by your league. Athletes with special needs due to medical conditions should also be noted and proper procedures indicated should they become suddenly afflicted.

Your first-aid kit should be equipped to handle minor injuries such as scrapes, strains, and bruises. More serious injuries, such as dislocations and broken bones, should be left to paramedics. Head, neck, and back injuries that result in loss of consciousness, numbness, or sharp pain should be considered very serious, and no attempt should be made to move the athlete. Make her as comfortable as you can, and wait for paramedics to arrive.

All injuries should be reported directly to you. Have a procedure for dealing with an injury, should one occur. Minor injuries, such as an abrasion of the knee or elbow, can be handled with a thorough cleaning using an antiseptic wipe. But what if the injury is a serious one, and you aren't a certified paramedic? You should have an emergency procedure established that all coaches and parents should know. Write it down and keep it in a first-aid kit, because when serious accidents happen, people tend to panic.

As the coach, it is your responsibility to manage risk. Although some risk is inherent in playing softball, you must fulfill your legal duties by conducting your team in a manner that is considered safe for your athletes and others. If you fail to perform your legal duty, then you may be considered negligent and open to a lawsuit should an injury occur. Make every effort to protect and care about your athletes and insist that your coaches do the same.

If you decide to coach a girl's softball team, you won't be doing it for the money. You'll be doing it because you love kids and softball, and you're willing to spend a large chunk of your free time teaching them how to play. You must not equate success with winning, but know that success comes through achieving a favorable outcome. Your basic role is to make sure that the players have a positive experience through participation on your team.

As a coach you will have a tremendous influence on shaping the lives of impressionable children who will seek guidance from you on the field of play. Your leadership ability, coaching style, and the things you do in running the team will likely leave a lasting impression on your athletes. Know your responsibilities with regard to the health and safety issues of your players and understand your liabilities as a coach. Provide your kids with a positive experience, and everyone on your team will benefit.

2

STRATEGIES FOR COACHING THE YOUNG FEMALE ATHLETE

YOU'VE PROBABLY HEARD that "knowledge is power." In a way that makes sense; if you "know all," then you should be able to influence people, move markets, and always remain one step ahead of everybody else. But what good is knowledge if you can't effectively get what you know across to anyone else? And what good is knowledge in coaching if you can't get what you know across to your players?

Regardless of how much information you possess, effective coaching always comes down to how well you transmit that information to your athletes. Strong communication skills are absolutely essential to the smooth and efficient operation of any softball team, at any level. And communication isn't limited to telling your athletes what time practice starts. Effective communication in coaching takes on many forms and is a critical component in team dynamics.

Your ability to teach the sport and its various component skills will factor heavily into how you will be viewed as a coach. You will need an understanding of fundamental teaching methods involved in motor skill learning and which strategies are best used in certain situations. You will need strategies for maintaining team discipline and motivating your athletes. Without discipline, chaos will likely reign and you will lose the respect of your athletes. Motivational strategies are of critical importance in keeping the experience fun for everyone involved. And ultimately, how you act as a person will shape the lives of your young athletes in ways that you'll perhaps never fully come to know.

EFFECTIVE COMMUNICATION

Communication in coaching is often thought of as one-way from coach to player. The coach often gives instructions to an athlete for proper skill execution, or explains the details of the next drill to be performed. But the coach who believes that he or she should operate like a "commander in chief" is doomed to failure. There's more to communication in sport than just shouting out orders. Even if you just silently stand with arms folded across your chest, you may not realize it, but you have just communicated quite a lot.

Coaches have different ways of communicating to athletes, and athletes respond differently to the various kinds of communication used. Some coaches scream and shout, while others do a lot of "talking" with body language and gesturing. One of the consistent themes in the female sport experience is that young girls play sports to build relationships with others. They want to develop personal relationships with their coaches and prefer open communication and empathy. Young girls need encouragement to build self-esteem and tend to perform better with positive feedback.

Coaching Tip

Pay attention to how your athletes act toward one another. Encourage them to help each other and not to criticize a teammate's performance. Positive communication between team members will build team unity!

Effective Communication with Players

There are several forms of communication. There is verbal communication, or the act of speaking to someone, and there is nonverbal communication, whereby messages are sent by way of body positions or facial gestures. According to Rainer Martens in *Successful Coaching,* it is estimated that 70 percent of all communication is nonverbal. Verbal communication contains both content and emotion. Content pertains to the actual meaning behind the words being said, while emotion has to do with how something is being said. Coaches often find themselves communicating in emotion-packed situations, and great care must be given to monitor self-control in watching not only what is said, but also how it is said.

When communicating verbally with your players, keep in mind that harsh criticism can destroy kids. According to T. Stenberg Horn in *Applied Sports Psychology: Personal Growth to Peak Performance*, research shows that the self-perceptions of younger children (those under the age of 10) are based, to a large extent, on the feedback of significant adults. That is, they likely view themselves as "good" or "bad" at a sport based on what parents, coaches, or teachers say to them. Kids need encouragement and positive feedback. Of course they make mistakes; that's part of the learning process. Instead of telling them what they did wrong, tell them how to do it right. And give them praise when they do it right.

Nonverbal communication, although silent by definition, can send a thousand messages and be more powerful than the spoken word. Because nothing is said, facial gestures and body positions are left to interpretation, and this sometimes leaves uncertainty about what was meant. Your players will "listen" to your nonverbal communication as well as to that of their teammates. To avoid problems with interpretations, it may be necessary to hold meetings where coaches and players can clear up any miscommunication.

For example, over the years, my athletes have spoken with me about our team chemistry on the bench during ballgames. Some are concerned about the "quiet types," those players who refrain from cheering and who just don't seem to care. Some athletes, although intensely into the game on an internal level, are outwardly quiet in the dugout. Their demeanor is the same whether the team is well in control of a game or down by one run with bases loaded. They remain focused on the game, and may even be standing at the fence, but they hardly say anything at all. Then there are the players who start every cheer in the dugout and are

Coaching Tip

When correcting a mistake, don't emphasize its bad effects. Instead, point out the good things that will happen if the athlete follows your instruction. Always balance criticism with praise.

literally hoarse from yelling by the end of the game. It is obvious to most members of the team that those who are yelling for their teammates are cheering in support of their efforts, and their verbal communication clearly shows as much. But at issue, it always seems, is the nonverbal communication of those players who are not as vocal. Their silence is often left open to interpretation, and that can be a difficult thing for some to manage. Clearly, at this point, it's time for a team meeting.

The team meeting is usually productive in that athletes share their views and observations. Ultimately, there are those who cheer and are very vocal about supporting their teammates, and there are those who support their teammates, but are not as vocal about it. Some players admit that they're just not "cheerleaders." Both sides, having had a chance to understand the other's point of view, accept the differences between them and move on. The team meeting lets teammates know that everyone was pulling for the good of the team.

Listening is also a part of communication. Taking the time to *hear* what another person is saying is important. Be sure you engage in active listening, whereby you repeat what has just been said to you, only you say it in your own words. This approach works best to clear up any misunderstandings immediately. Listening to athletes and parents, and allowing them to have input, is an important part of effective communication in coaching.

Effective Communication with Parents

When I was gathering research for this book, I ran across SportsParents.com, a Web site for parents and coaches of young ath-

---

CAPTAINS' MEETINGS

Have the team elect captains and hold regular captains' meetings. Your captains will know a good deal of what is going on with individual players and your team. They will be able to give you insights and thoughts about the direction in which the program is heading. Keep what is said at captains' meetings confidential. Otherwise you risk alienating the captains from their teammates and thus losing an important line of communication to the team.

letes. There was a particular piece entitled, "When You're the Coach, the Kids on the Team Are Sometimes the Least of Your Problems." The article described "nightmare parents" and listed categories of parent types, such as "The Screamer," "The Whiner," "The Interfering Parent," the "Must-Win Parent," and several more. The article gave straightforward suggestions for coaches on how to handle the kinds of parents referenced in each particular category. To be sure, those parents are out there. As the coach, set the tone early in the season by conducting a parent meeting before your team's first practice. Doing so will help you develop a positive relationship with your athletes' parents, as well as avoid some of the pitfalls of parental involvement in youth sports today. (Serious issues and dealing with parents are discussed in chapter 3.)

Coaching Tip

Avoid constant instruction. Give athletes time to get into the flow of the activity and enjoy completing the task. Give instructions at the start about what is to be accomplished. Make only one or two comments as feedback on their performance.

Building positive relationships with parents is almost as important as the relationships you build with your athletes. A parent meeting will help you get off to a good start. Whether or not you include the athletes in your first parent meeting is up to you. Determine a convenient time and place for parents to attend, and contact all of the parents, either by phone or by personal letter. Plan for no more than two hours, and take the time to plan your agenda.

The items on your agenda should include, but not be limited to:

- Brief introduction and background of yourself, assistant coaches, and any additional staff
- Goals and objectives for the season
- Your coaching style and philosophy
- How you run a typical practice
- What you expect from your athletes (rules)
- What you expect from the parents
- Risks involved in the sport, insurance information, and league policies
- Practice and game schedule

- Required equipment
- Parents' question-and-answer period

Be organized in your presentation and firm in your tone when addressing the group. Be attentive to their questions and show compassion when answering them. Parents can be your greatest allies or your worst nightmares.

Effective communication is a critical element in building and maintaining positive relationships among coaches, players, and parents. Listening to others, and allowing others to have input, provides the coach with additional information that can be useful in determining the best possible direction for an individual or the program. Don't let the initial parent meeting be the end of communication with parents. Make the effort to stay connected as the season progresses. On occasion, ask the parents how their kids are doing and how their daughters like being on the team. Doing so demonstrates that you care about the athletes and, at the same time, shows that you're available should they have any concerns they wish to discuss with you.

EFFECTIVE TEACHING

Effective coaching involves the ability to teach kids how to play softball. You must not only know proper execution of such skills as throwing, batting, fielding, and sliding, but you must also know which teaching techniques are most beneficial and under what circumstances. Learn the proper skills, and learn how to develop pro-

---

PARENT GUIDELINES

Establish behavioral guidelines for parents to follow during ballgames. Parents should refrain from coaching their daughters and yelling negative things, but should instead praise the effort and not get caught up in the outcome. Ask parents not to talk to their child on the bench while a game is in progress. The child needs to be focused on the field of play, and not be distracted by friends or family.

DIFFERENT LEVELS OF PLAY

You will likely find yourself with players of varying skill levels on your team. Encourage positive verbal interaction between teammates. Be aware of skilled athletes who criticize or make fun of those who are less skilled. Emphasize the contributions of all members of the team. When conducting drills, use small groups with two lesser skilled players for every one player with more advanced skills. Refrain from referring to lesser skilled athletes as substitutes, back-up players, or second team players. If you divide up your team to scrimmage, use the terms blue team, red team, and so on.

gressions for teaching those skills. In providing a positive experience for your athletes, structure their learning for success. Give them an opportunity to succeed and watch them grow!

When I work with my athletes on the field, my coaching, or teaching, is geared to their age level. After nearly 20 years of coaching major college softball, I have developed an understanding and expectation of where my college softball players should be, both mentally and physically. For example, my athletes must have a high degree of proficiency in nearly all of the physical skills associated with the sport. We, therefore, spend time at practice working on the refinement of those skills in the physical domain, in addition to focusing on the various mental strategies at work internally that affect their performances. When I talk about a skill or technique, I use words and concepts that an 18-year-old athlete will understand. But if I were working with a 10-year-old softball player, I wouldn't use a word like "parallel," or expect her to grasp the concept of "opening up 180 degrees." Likewise, I wouldn't expect a team of 10-year-olds to understand an explanation of how to run a first and third situation defensively, because those words and concepts are beyond their level of comprehension in explanation form. Simply put, 10-year-olds are just not ready yet!

This section covers effective teaching methods. Effective teaching means getting your athletes to learn what it is you want them to know. Be aware that you must gear these methods to the age level with which you are working. A 13-year-old will be more advanced than a 7-year-old will, both in skill development and in the ability to understand your language and comprehend concepts that are being introduced. Even within a group of 7-year-olds, you may see varying degrees of development and comprehension. A first-grade teacher deals with the same element in the classroom. The only difference is your classroom happens to be the softball diamond.

Knowing your athletes' levels of understanding and comprehension will help make you an effective teacher. Younger athletes (ages 7 to 8) should focus on the basics of softball, such as throwing, catching, tee hitting, running to first base, and throwing to first for an out. As they grow older, more complex skills can be introduced. It is important to allow your athletes to be successful, and keep the sport interesting by introducing new skills when you think they are ready. Some girls may immediately grasp new skills or concepts of the game, while others may struggle a bit. Trial and error on your part is okay. If you find your athletes are not ready to grasp a new skill or strategy, try to develop a progression or lead-up activity with parts of the new skill or strategy, and introduce it in a different way next time.

When teaching a new skill, kids learn best if they see a demonstration in addition to hearing an explanation of how a movement should be executed. A demonstration gives kids a clear picture of what the skill should look like. You should have your athletes standing or seated comfortably in an area without distraction and positioned so that all can see you. If you are unable to demonstrate the skill correctly, have someone proficient perform the movement. Before the demonstration begins, name the skill and explain its significance to the game of softball. Begin the demonstration and point out specific areas of emphasis as the skill is performed. Repeat the demonstration several times. Ask the athletes if they have any questions. Then ask your own questions to further clarify and make sure they understand the objective of the skill or movement.

It is important to have your athletes practice the skill as soon after the demonstration as possible.

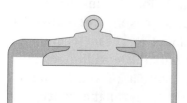

Coaching Tip

Allow older kids freedom to make some decisions in games, such as calling plays independently of the coaching staff.

You should have multiple practice stations set up in advance so that athletes are not standing around. Idle athletes will lose interest quickly and will begin to be a distraction for those who are trying to practice. Explain the stations, and demonstrate the movement to be performed at each station, if necessary. Emphasize what it is you want your players to accomplish.

Coaching Tip

Talk about good sportsmanship. Ask your players to give examples of good and poor sportsmanship. Set a team goal of exhibiting five behaviors of good sportsmanship at the next practice or game.

Providing constructive feedback to your athletes is a vital part of the teaching process. It is your job, as the coach, to evaluate each athlete's performance, and to let her know how she is doing. Praise her if she is doing it well, and tell her how to do it right if she is performing the skill incorrectly. Be positive and give encouragement.

If you have the time and the technology, you may want to videotape your athletes. Although this can be time-consuming, it can be very instrumental in providing athletes with constructive feedback in the more complex skills, such as batting. Batting is a skill that is performed at such a high rate of speed that it is often difficult to tell exactly what is happening at certain points in the swing without the aid of slow-motion videography. Another advantage of video is it helps an athlete see something in her swing that you have pointed out that needs correcting, but that she is having a hard time either "seeing" or believing. It's hard to argue with something caught on camera!

Another aspect of effective teaching has to do with "whole" or "part" learning. Whole learning is teaching a skill in its entirety, all at once. Part learning is breaking down the skill into smaller pieces or components and teaching each piece, one by one, usually over time. Whole learning is a more effective teaching method for motor skills that are relatively simple, such as catching a ball. More complex motor skills, such as sliding into a base or batting, can best be taught by the part learning method. In the Sliding Drills box, you can see how sliding into a base is broken down into five parts, each taught separately. A progression is established that allows players to focus on smaller pieces of the whole.

Gear your teaching to the level of your athletes, and don't be afraid to introduce new skills to see if they're ready to progress in development. Adjust what you teach to the various levels of development within your own team, while keeping practice activities fun, rewarding, and challenging. Break down more complex skills into components, and teach them gradually over time. Being a good coach means being a good teacher!

SLIDING DRILLS

Here is an example of the "part" learning method used to teach sliding into a base.

Part 1 (Day 1): Correct Body Position for Sliding

Athletes should sit on the ground (preferably grass) with both legs extended straight out in front of them and hands in their laps. Tell them to keep the right leg straight and bend the left leg so that it lies on the ground on its side, with the left foot positioned just below the right knee. Have athletes lean back, almost lying on the ground, and raise both arms up and behind them into the air, palms of the hands facing out. Explain that this is the correct body position when actually sliding feet first. Have the athletes stand up. Announce to the team that when you yell, "Get down!" you want them to drop to the correct sitting position for sliding feet first. Now yell, "Get down!" so that everyone can hear you. Check to make sure that they have all dropped into the correct body position. Repeat this drill several times until they get into the proper sliding position consistently on their own.

Part 2 (Day 2)

Review the correct sitting position. Have athletes form a circle with at least two body lengths of distance between them. Have them all face in the same direction and begin walking around in a circle, keeping the same distance between them. When you yell, "Get down!" they must drop to the correct sit-

TEAM DISCIPLINE

"Practice starts at 6:00 P.M. sharp on Thursday!" That's what you told your team last Tuesday. Now it's Thursday, 6:15 P.M., and half of your players still haven't shown up for practice. Perfect timing, too! You had planned on a little intrasquad scrimmage, and you need to have everyone present to make two teams. Besides, it starts getting dark near 8:00. Great, now you'll have to wing it. What is the matter with this team?

The answer may lie in team discipline. Orderly conduct is necessary for the smooth running of any team. At Sacramento State, I

ting position for sliding feet first. Have them stay put until you can check each athlete's body position. Do this drill several times until they drop into the proper sliding position consistently.

Part 3 (continued on Day 2)

With athletes in a circle, and at least two body lengths of distance between them, have them go from walking to a slow jog. When you yell, "Get down!" they must drop to the correct sitting position for sliding feet first. Proceed as above. Repeat this drill several times until they get into the proper sliding position consistently from a slow jog. For each repetition of the drill, keep the formation the same but add more speed to the jogging. You don't want the athletes to get hurt.

Part 4 (Day 3)

When athletes have mastered the skill to this point, take them to running full speed and sliding on a slip and slide (this is especially fun when it's hot outside).

Part 5 (Day 4)

Cut out large pieces of cardboard and lay them in the baseline in front of the base. Make sure athletes wear sweat pants or have their legs covered so they don't get burns from the cardboard. Your objective is to find ways to eliminate the fear of getting hurt associated with sliding.

DIRT FROM THE DIAMOND

Laura Norwood coaches the 12 and under California Grapettes out of Stockton, California. She has been coaching for 19 years and really enjoys the younger players. She likes the competitive nature of ASA travel ball, and her teams have finished as high as ninth nationally. Laura feels it is absolutely necessary to have team rules.

Because her team travels quite often, Laura has rules that pertain to expectations of players when on the road or when appearing in tournaments. Her athletes must wear dresses when flying, be in their own rooms for bed check when staying at a hotel, stay out of the swimming pool, and, although the Grapettes organization pays for dinner on the road, leave a one-dollar tip when eating out. Laura sees the rules as part of the learning process in teaching them how to be responsible as they continue to grow and mature.

have a seven-page team policy that covers program rules so that my athletes know what is expected of them. In addition to the rules themselves, I also include the consequences of breaking such rules. By including consequences or penalties, I have taken the subjectivity out of rules enforcement. This enables me to be fair and consistent in dealing with my athletes.

Rules should be simple for younger children and get more complex for older athletes. You will want to establish simple rules for things like attendance at games and practices, tardiness, required clothing when practicing and playing, and behavior during practice and competition. As athletes get older, you may want to add rules for behavior toward teammates and officials, rules for having visitors at practice or games, and rules for drugs and alcohol.

Team rules should be established that reflect your expectations of the athletes in their specific environment. For example, if you conduct a team whose responsibilities are limited to attendance at practices and games only at one site, then simple rules should suffice. If, however, your team is involved in more extensive travel, then you will want to expand on your rules to incorporate what expectations you may have of them on the road.

Once you make up the rules, setting the consequences or establishing penalties for breaking the rules will be the next step. For the penalty to be effective, it must be meaningful to the athlete. Holding the player out of a game or practice would be a meaningful consequence. Be sure you equate the penalty with the severity of the rules infraction, however. If a child misses practice without notifying you, then holding her out of the next competition or not allowing her to start the next game might be an appropriate consequence. If, however, you keep her out of competition for several games, you may be viewed as being too harsh.

Once you have a set of rules and penalties, you will be expected to be consistent in enforcing them and applying them fairly. When you hold your players accountable for their actions, you teach them respect for rules and responsibility. Write the rules and give everyone a copy. Allow older players to get involved in creating the team rules and ask them for ideas on appropriate penalties. Explain the rules at the beginning of the season and answer any questions that your players or their parents may ask. Make sure everybody understands what is expected of him or her.

MOTIVATING ATHLETES

Why do kids play sports, or better yet, why do girls play softball? Research shows that kids are socialized and learn valuable lessons about life through sport. But kids don't choose to play because of the life lessons they'll learn. They choose to play sports for other reasons. Understanding why kids play sports in the first place will help you keep them motivated to play so that they will learn values important to our society.

> ### Coaching Tip
> Player input is usually appropriate for kids ages 10 and older. Ask your team what appropriate rules and penalties might be to find out what is meaningful to them.

A 1977 study conducted by the Youth Sports Institute at Michigan State University found the top five reasons kids played sports were:

1. To have fun
2. To improve skills and learn new ones

3. For thrills and excitement
4. To be with friends or make new friends
5. To succeed or win

A good softball coach who understands the athletes' reasons for playing the game will strive to plan activities and practices that meet the athletes' goals.

It is also important to understand why kids drop out of sports. These reasons allow coaches to structure activities in the program to avoid the things that drive youth from participation. In the Youth Sports Institute Survey, conducted by Michigan State University, the top five reasons children dropped out of sports, listed by gender, were:

TOP FIVE REASONS BOYS DROPPED OUT

1. I was no longer interested
2. It was no longer fun
3. The sport took too much time
4. The coach played favorites
5. The coach was a poor teacher

WHY WE PLAY THE GAME

Plan activities at practice that incorporate the five reasons kids play sports. Some ideas might include:

1. Turn sprints for warm-ups into relay races between teams or make a game of "tag" a conditioning activity (FUN).

2. Introduce a new drill or skill at each practice (IMPROVE SKILLS/LEARN NEW ONES).

3. Practice sliding on a hot day on a slip and slide (THRILLS/EXCITEMENT).

4. During stretching, before practice, go around the team and have each athlete say what her favorite food, color, animal, etc., is (MAKE NEW FRIENDS/BE WITH FRIENDS).

5. On a hot day after practice, reward the team with Popsicles if they worked hard (SUCCEED/WIN).

TOP FIVE REASONS GIRLS DROPPED OUT

1. I was no longer interested
2. It was no longer fun
3. I needed more time to study
4. There was too much pressure
5. The coach was a poor teacher

Although softball is a team sport, your athletes are individuals and may have more specific reasons for playing on the team. Take time to talk with your athletes individually and as a team, and ask them why they chose to play. You can tailor your motivational strategies to help reinforce the things that are important to each of them in helping them enjoy their participation. Remember, what motivates one may not motivate another.

Athletes often view ballgames as the fun part of being on a team. Make sure all your athletes get a chance to play and be involved in the game. Although only nine players can be on the field at any one time, players on the bench should be encouraged to watch teammates who play their positions so that they may learn from others. It also helps to stay focused on the game to learn about the strengths and weaknesses of the opponent so that when it is time for the athlete to enter into the contest, she knows what is going on.

Games aren't the only place to have fun, however. Practices can be fun, too. Keep all your players involved in drills and activities and not just standing around. Vary your practices by introducing new drills and new challenges. Keep drills challenging but attainable. If they are too easy, your athletes will get bored easily and become unmotivated. Likewise, if they are too difficult, athletes may get frustrated and decide to quit.

Applaud effort and focus on the process, not the outcome. It is important to keep the proper perspective on a child's participation in the sport. Make sure that winning doesn't equal success and losing doesn't equal failure. According to Rainer Martens in *Successful Coaching,* success must be seen in terms of athletes exceeding their own goals rather than surpassing the performance of others. Help athletes set realistic goals; structure drills and activities in an effort to help athletes succeed. In this way, players will be focused on maximizing their efforts for self-improvement instead of focusing on comparisons with others.

Rewards can be a powerful tool in motivating an athlete. According to Ronald E. Smith in *Applied Sport Psychology: Personal Growth to Peak Performance,* when people are motivated to perform an activity for its own sake, they are said to be intrinsically motivated. When they perform some activity only for an external reward, they are said to be extrinsically motivated. When young kids first decide to try a sport, they are intrinsically motivated. They do it for the sake of the activity. Later, as team sports get more sophisticated, ribbons, medals, certificates of achievement, and other awards enter into the picture and athletes may become extrinsically motivated. Research is mixed as to the effectiveness of giving external rewards for an activity that is already intrinsically motivating. Some critics of external rewards feel that this system actually diminishes the intrinsic motivational level of the athlete, and eventually, the athlete loses her desire to play and drops out. Proponents, on the other hand, argue that external rewards enhance intrinsic motivation in athletes, often enabling them to achieve new heights.

The best rewards may still be "free." As a coach, you can use rewards such as a pat on the back, a smile, a head nod, or simple applause to help motivate your athletes. Stay positive in your approach and do everything you can to make the athlete feel worthy.

Motivational strategies that incorporate why kids play sports will keep them having fun and will meet their needs for participating in the first place. If everyone is involved in activities at practices and games, they will be less likely to lose interest and drop out. Emphasize the importance of giving one's best effort, and focus on the attainment of personal goals as a measure of success. Losing, in itself, is not failure, and it is important to make sure that kids see the difference. Use external rewards sparingly and when you do use them, be generous with those that are free.

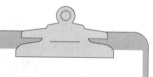

Coaching Tip

To help athletes view success in terms of self-improvement, teach them to set realistic goals, such as throwing to a base without an error or holding onto the ball with two hands for each catch.

BEING A GOOD ROLE MODEL

Take a moment to reflect on your life and think of one or two adults who positively influenced you most dramatically while growing up. Were they teachers? Coaches? Were they your parents, or somebody else's? Whatever the case, I'll bet they were people you aspired to be like. Chances are, they were good role models.

A good role model is someone who exhibits the behaviors and actions highly valued in our society. A role model is somebody we look up to, usually somebody we greatly admire and respect as an individual. Trying to pattern our own behavior after a role model is a desirable choice. The minute you become a coach, you become a role model for your players.

How you act as an individual will say a lot about you as a coach. Just like your athletes, you are a human being first and a coach second. The sports domain is filled with strong emotions when faced with tough situations, and it is important to keep everything in perspective. When you work with children, you are in a position to shape the lives of very young and impressionable little people. They will become big people some day, and the way you act and the things you say now will likely leave an impression on them that will last a lifetime. When you leave that impression, do everything you can to make sure you leave a positive mark on their development.

As a coach, you will be responsible for your athletes' personal, social, and psychological development to some degree. It is up to you to guide them in this socialization process. Not only how you act, but also what you do about the way they act, will be consequential. Positive role models have the following traits.

PERSONAL TRAITS
- Honest
- Moral
- Ethical
- Positive
- Compassionate

- Influential
- Responsible
- Disciplined

SOCIAL SKILLS

- Good sportsmanship
- Cooperative
- Respect for authority
- Respect for others
- Respect for property

PSYCHOLOGICAL DEVELOPMENT

- High degree of self-esteem
- Self-confident
- Self-respecting

As a coach, it is incumbent upon you to model desirable behavior. When your athletes observe you applauding the effort and skill of an opponent making a great play, your athletes will follow your example. If you yell and whine about an umpire's poor call, your athletes will yell and whine at the umpire as well. Be sure to set a good example. Avoid being the coach whose motto is "Do as I say, not as I do." A team is a reflection of the coach, and your team's behavior is a likely indicator of yours.

In addition to modeling appropriate behavior, be prepared to intervene when you observe your players exhibiting inappropriate behavior. Talk with your team about things like sportsmanship and behavior that is considered good and that which is considered unacceptable. Make sure your athletes know the consequences of their behavior when they conduct themselves poorly. If one of your players uses foul language after committing an error, pull the athlete aside and be firm in explaining that use of such language is unacceptable and that if it happens again, she will not play. Similarly, if you overhear an athlete say something derogatory to a

Coaching Tip

Praise athletes when they exhibit proper social skills, such as when a player helps a teammate onto her feet after a play. Applaud the other team when they make a good play. Praise your athletes for doing the same.

teammate, opponent, or official, you should talk to the athlete privately and let her know her behavior will not be tolerated on your team. Advise her that if the behavior is repeated, she will not play. In situations such as these, act as soon as possible after the occurrence, or your intervention is likely to lose some of its impact.

Coaching Tip

The best way to motivate players and reinforce good behavior is to reward them when they exhibit good behavior. A pat on the back, a word of acknowledgment, or just a sign that you noticed will encourage them to repeat the good behavior.

Once you have decided to become a coach, you must learn how to coach effectively. Strategies for coaching include learning how to communicate with players and parents, how to teach effectively, and how to maintain team discipline. Taking the time to learn why kids play sports will give you insights into how to keep them motivated to play. And because you are in a position to influence children, you must constantly be aware of what it means to be a good role model. Teach your kids well, for they will be a reflection of you.

3

COACHING GIRLS

THERE'S NOT MUCH research on whether girls are coached differently from boys. Yet, in talking with youth coaches who have worked with children of both genders, there is widespread agreement that boys and girls are coached differently. In American society, girls and boys are socialized differently and learn gender roles early in life. As they grow older and their bodies begin to change and develop physically, society's expectations of girls and boys begin to play a larger role in their social and psychological development.

Girls and boys experience sport differently. Girls value sport primarily for social reasons, such as making new friends and being with others. Boys, on the other hand, value sport to learn skills; building camaraderie is secondary. Later, as boys and girls grow and biologically mature, physical changes such as increases in body size and weight begin to have an effect on the coordination of skills and on changes in sport performance. These physical changes during adolescence are often accompanied by psychological changes as boys and girls learn to deal with their own perceived competence and the pressures of societal expectations.

Adolescence can be a difficult time for young female athletes. Conscientious coaches must be aware of serious issues likely to affect their young players, such as eating disorders, parental pressures, competitive stress, and sexual harassment. As a coach, be aware of the special needs and considerations of pubescent female athletes so that you can be better prepared to provide a positive experience for them during this crucial period.

HOW GIRLS AND BOYS PLAY SPORTS

Most fundamental motor skills, such as running, jumping, throwing, and catching, will be developed in children by the ages of 6 or 7. If a child doesn't master overhand throwing by age 7, for example, then a proficient motor pattern in throwing may never be fully realized. There is evidence of this in schoolyards across America—particularly with girls whose mastery in overhand throwing is not fully achieved. The classic pattern exhibited in this case is when the throw is executed by stepping forward with the leg that is on the same side of the body as the throwing arm—thus the cliché, "throwing like a girl." Research between genders seems to indicate some differences in abilities at an early age. According to Numminen and Saakslahti, boys excel at skills that require speed, muscular strength, and endurance, while girls tend to excel when balance and flexibility are needed.

In preadolescence (ages 6 to 10), children begin to become aware of their own abilities in the physical, social, and cognitive domain. Sports participation in the preadolescent years can provide children with the opportunity to learn and develop more complex motor skills of specific sports and provide opportunities for social interaction with friends. In preadolescent children, it is important to focus on basic skills and knowledge of the game of softball, in addition to the athletes' personal and social development. Table 3.1 shows some suggested areas of focus.

As athletes grow older, more complex sport skills and strategies involving multiple players may be introduced along with more complex rules of the game. For example, rundowns, first and third situations, and an understanding of the infield fly rule may be introduced once the fundamentals have been mastered. It is also appropriate to begin to introduce conditioning activities to enhance physical skill development.

Table 3.1	Suggested personal and social skills to focus on when coaching softball skills		

Softball Skills	Personal Skills	Social Skills
Throwing	Attitude	Respect for authority
Catching	Best effort	Respect for others
Tee/controlled pitch hitting	Listening	Care of equipment
Basic fielding techniques	Following directions	Sportsmanship
Simple baserunning	Self-respect	Teamwork
General position play	Cleanliness	Pride in team
Basic rules of the game	Responsibility	Sharing

Taken from Paul Vogel, *Youth Softball: A Complete Handbook* (1992)

According to Caroline Silby in *Games Girls Play,* there is a tendency for young girls to see themselves as responsible for failure in sport performance while boys tend to focus on external circumstances as a reason for failure. A girl may view her unsuccessful attempts to get on base in a game as the result of her clumsiness, while a boy tends to see the opposing pitcher as having a great day on the mound as the reason for his unsuccessful attempts to get on base. This tendency toward external focus in boys may help to keep them motivated and involved in sport longer, so that they eventually

GIVE THEM A COOKIE!

Be generous with praise. Give her a "cookie"! Just like a cream-filled cookie has a filling in between two crispy wafers, you can give instruction in between two comments of encouragement. When Susie strikes out at bat, say, "Gee, Susie, you had a great swing up there at bat. Next time keep your eye on the ball, and you'll get a hit. Hitting isn't easy, but you're doing a great job with the swing!" Use the cookie paradigm to praise your athletes when you see they are frustrated.

come to experience success. When coaching young girls, it is important to provide encouragement and inspire them to persist.

PHYSICAL DIFFERENCES BETWEEN BOYS AND GIRLS

Early adolescence is usually a time of dramatic physical changes, as well as psychological and emotional. Besides the physical changes in body size and weight, puberty, the period of late childhood when biological changes take place in boys and girls as they transition through adolescence, spells the onset of biological maturity for boys and girls as sexual characteristics begin to emerge.

Hormones influence rapid growth and trigger changes in the development of sexual organs and other characteristics that are gender specific. This transition from childhood to adulthood varies not only between boys and girls, but among them as well.

Between ages 9 to 14, boys and girls begin to mature sexually. In addition to increases in height and weight, boys experience physical changes as a result of testosterone, commonly considered the male hormone, which is responsible for muscle growth, body and facial hair, and other male sex characteristics. These changes often

COACHING ADOLESCENT GIRLS

If you coach girls ages 10 and up, be prepared for the possibility of one of your athletes starting her period while playing softball. Menarche can appear at any time with this age group and can be very traumatic for some individuals. Be sure to carry individually wrapped sanitary napkins in the first-aid kit so that if an emergency arises, you will be prepared. Sudden bleeding may catch the athlete by surprise, and she should be assisted to the nearest bathroom with the necessary supplies from your kit. If you are a male coach and not comfortable with this situation, talk with a female coach or female manager on your staff before the situation arises. If you don't have a female on your staff, consider adding one. Otherwise, talk with a female parent who attends a large percentage of games and practices, and ask for her assistance if necessary.

provide boys with renewed self-confidence and self-esteem as increases in strength and speed result in a kind of new physical prowess, often advantageous to sports performance.

Girls also experience height and weight gains, as well as biological changes. Girls' biological changes are a result of estrogen, a hormone that causes the growth of breasts and other female sex characteristics and that regulates menstruation. Menarche, or the first menstrual period, is a significant event in the life of an adolescent female. It often signals a change in

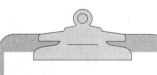

Coaching Tip
Fluctuating hormones cause the menstrual cycle. As a result, females may experience changes in moods and emotions. During this time, extra patience and understanding will help to ease the situation.

expectations that society has for a young girl as she begins to enter womanhood. Young girls may experience menarche as early as age 10, and coaches must be prepared to handle the situation should it arise while they are involved in the team environment.

"Childhood Experience and the Onset of Menarche: A Test of a Sociobiological Model" explains that with the onset of menarche, uncertainty about the changes and growth that a young girl experiences can be unsettling. It is a critical time in a young adolescent's life for the reorganization of her body image and sexual identity. Menarche occurs at different times for different girls. According to *Periods, From Menarche to Menopause,* there are indications that girls who begin to develop earlier than their peers experience increased levels of stress because they look older and tend to become involved in more sexual relationships. This often results in unwanted attention due to teasing and ridicule, which leads to embarrassment and self-consciousness.

The emotional and social stresses brought about by puberty can be challenging for young girls participating in sports activities. As the young female body develops, biological changes cause physical changes in body proportion, and the young female athlete may struggle with her sports performance. Increasing hip width and upper body development will change the young athlete's center of gravity.

As she learns to compensate athletically for these changes, she is met with societal expectations of what her body should look like as well. This period of time can be quite frustrating and overwhelming.

Be aware of behavioral changes in your athletes. If you observe those who don't appear to be optimistic, or who appear to be losing their self-confidence while their performance suffers, give them encouragement. Discuss how they are feeling about themselves and ask them about the change in behavior. Structure drills and activities for success and model correct performance. You may want to decrease competitive situations during this time and work with players to build self-confidence. Encouragement can be empowering to young athletes struggling with insecurities, and you can play a powerful part in this process.

PSYCHOLOGICAL DIFFERENCES BETWEEN BOYS AND GIRLS

The mental and emotional processes involved in the psychological domain of boys' and girls' participation in sports is large in scope. In addition to the biological maturation process, perceived competence, peer relationships, and social expectations play a major role in a child's endeavor to engage in physical activity. An awareness and understanding of these influences will help you to structure the participation experience for positive outcomes.

We know that the primary reason kids play sports is to have fun. Other reasons are to improve skills and learn new ones, for the thrill and excitement, to be with friends and make new ones, and to succeed and win. Sport is one of the few areas where kids can actively participate in something that can result in meaningful consequences for themselves, their friends and family, and the community. It is no wonder that millions of kids participate in some kind of physical activity in the United States alone.

Children's perceptions of their ability to learn and perform sport skills have much to do with whether they continue to play or drop out. According to "Motivational Orientations in Sports," children with higher levels of perceived competence in sport skills tend to participate longer than those children with lower levels. As a coach, you can enhance a child's perceived competence in a skill by helping her evaluate her own self-improvement rather than by focusing on the outcome of winning the contest.

One of the major reasons kids play sports is affiliation. Jay Coakley explains that the emphasis on same-sex peer groups and having best friends is characteristic of preadolescence. In this stage of development, it is important for kids to discover similarities and differences between themselves and each other, and to begin to establish individuality. It is this process that helps kids learn more about right and wrong, good and bad, and it allows them to learn more about other people.

Females are more apt to value friendship in sports participation. In a 1996 study conducted by Weiss and others, girls viewed emotional support as a benefit of having friendships in sport. Peer relationships play an important role in a young girl's motivation to be involved in physical activity, suggesting that promoting activities that enhance friendships among girls on the team will be highly valued.

Societal expectations of how a woman should look have tremendous implications for the mental and emotional states of young female athletes. The ideal woman, by society's standard, is beautiful and has a slender, lean physique. Consequently, young girls are particularly concerned with being beautiful and maintaining a thin body type. Even though males have an implied ideal body image of size, strength, and power, a study by Diane L. Gill shows that girls and women are more prone to view their bodies negatively. Given such expectations for women, it's not hard to see how navigation through adolescence can be challenging for a young girl.

Coaches who pay particular attention to psychological factors and

Coaching Tip

Plan team activities or get-togethers outside of practice and games to enhance peer relationships. A pizza party or team barbecue is a great way to get the team together to have fun and allow the girls to hang out with friends.

how they affect young female athletes are better able to guide and assist them to have a positive experience in sports participation. An athlete's perceived competence in the sport will likely play a major role in the longevity of her participation.

SERIOUS ISSUES IN SOFTBALL TODAY

As young girls try to balance changes in their bodies with societal expectations, coaches should pay particular attention to those athletes exhibiting signs of distress. There's growing evidence of a dark side in youth sports today. Youth sport coaches must be aware of the potentially negative impact of the youth sports experience. Have you ever wondered how kids handle the stresses of competition? How are these stresses likely manifesting themselves in the lives of 8-, 9-, 10-, and 11-year-old children? Are you a male coach working with young girls? Can you imagine ever being accused of sexual harassment? What steps should you take to avoid ever being in that situation?

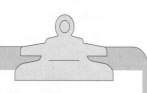

Coaching Tip

Help athletes focus on internal thinking, or the things they can control—goals, concentration, effort, and how to react to others. Get them away from an external focus, or stressful things they can't control—what others say or do, weather conditions, or umpires' calls.

You may have seen firsthand how vicious parents can be over a game involving children. Or perhaps you have read about parents fighting after a game, resulting in serious injury or even death. In extreme cases, you may have to deal with girls with eating disorders, a potentially life-threatening situation, or with girls who have been sexually harassed.

These issues are part of a growing concern of sport psychologists, educators, and youth sports proponents who are calling for change in the way youth sports are currently conducted in this country. There is a major movement calling for national certification programs to train coaches and educate parents on appropriate behavior and sportsmanship. As a coach, you should be aware of the more serious issues in the sport and know what steps to take to either prevent a bad situation from ever developing, or know what to do when you think one is underway.

Eating Disorders

Anorexia nervosa and bulimia are the two most common eating disorders. People with anorexia suffer from the intense fear of getting fat and severely restrict food intake. People with bulimia suffer from a disorder that involves bingeing and purging in which forced vomiting follows excessive eating. A third classification, which is beginning to receive widespread recognition, is called anorexia *athletica*. This condition describes the athlete who exercises constantly and is a fanatic about weight and diet. The athletes most affected by this disorder are females and are typically found in sports where form is important for success, such as gymnastics, figure skating, and diving.

Eating disorders place a great deal of stress on the body and, if left unchecked, may ultimately be fatal. In 1994, The Diagnostic and Statistical Manual of Mental Disorders identified the following characteristics of anorexia nervosa:

1. Weight loss that leads to a regularly maintained body weight of 15 percent below the expected norm.
2. Intense fear of gaining weight or becoming fat in spite of being underweight.
3. Disturbance of how one's body weight, size, or shape is experienced (e.g., feeling fat even when obviously underweight).
4. The absence of at least three consecutive menstrual cycles when they otherwise would have occurred.

One of the most difficult aspects of anorexia is that in severe cases, individuals afflicted with the disorder are unable to see themselves as abnormal.

People with bulimia, on the other hand, know they have a problem. A bulimic person may become depressed because of low self-esteem and may eat excessively in an effort to feel better. This excessive eating then leads to guilt, and the person attempts to purge the food with either forced vomiting or the use of laxatives. If left unchecked, bulimia may lead to anorexia. In 1994, the American Psychiatric Association identified the following characteristics for bulimia:

1. Repeated episodes of binge eating (successive periods of consuming large amounts of food).
2. A sense of lack of control over the eating behavior during binges.
3. Engaging regularly in self-induced vomiting, use of laxatives or diuretics, strict dieting or fasting, or vigorous exercise in order to prevent weight gain.
4. An average minimum of two binge-eating episodes a week for at least three months.
5. Persistent overconcerns with body shape and weight.

Eating disorders stem from psychological issues. Adolescent girls are especially vulnerable as changes in body shape, size, and weight may cause increased levels of self-consciousness. Young athletes who suffer from eating disorders usually have low self-esteem and believe their thoughts and feelings don't matter. Individuals who haven't learned how to satisfy their emotional needs in healthy ways may turn to eating disorders as coping mechanisms in an effort to gain control over something they can take charge of—their weight. Once the cycle starts, it is extremely difficult to break.

As a coach of female athletes, you should be aware of the Female Athlete Triad, as described in Caroline Silby's *Games Girls Play*. The American College of Sports Medicine identified three medical disorders that make up the triad: eating disorders, amenorrhea (no period for three or more consecutive months), and osteoporosis (bone loss). The three components are interrelated and not only have implications in the short term but also have long-term consequences for the health of the female athlete.

NUTRITION

Talk to your team about the importance of good nutrition and eating habits. Fruits make good snacks in between games or when hungry prior to physical activity. Encourage your athletes to drink water regularly. Provide information about eating disorders and be careful about what you say regarding players' weights. Never ridicule or make fun of an athlete's concerns about weight. Do not recommend weight loss or gain and never hold weigh-ins.

EATING DISORDERS

Signs of eating disorders may include amenorrhea, sudden weight loss, weight too low, denial of hunger, preoccupation with food or calories, disappearing after meals, and an obsession with dieting. If you suspect that an athlete may have an eating disorder, be supportive and empathetic, get help and advice from a specialist, make referrals to a specific person, and make sure you follow-up with the athlete to be sure she is getting professional help. An athlete with an eating disorder needs help.

The three components of the triad essentially have a domino effect on one another. As the athlete develops an eating disorder, the amount of calories consumed is less than what is required by the body in energy expenditure. Thus, the body interprets this negative energy balance as starvation and begins to shut down various internal systems. Specifically, the body shuts down the female reproduction capability, thereby stopping the menstrual cycle. When menstruation stops, the body's production of estrogen decreases. This decrease in estrogen, coupled with decreased dietary calcium intake later in life, may cause the bones to release calcium into the bloodstream to replace low levels. The result may be bone loss or osteoporosis.

Dealing with Parents

Parental over-involvement has become a big issue in youth sports today. Some of this behavior has even become abusive. Parents are coaching their kids from the stands, yelling at coaches, yelling at umpires, and provoking opponents' fans. One documented case of death involved a parent who knocked a youth hockey coach to the ice in Reading, Massachusetts, and repeatedly banged his head into the ice until he had no pulse. The coach died the next day.

As a college coach, I deal with softball parents. I happen to view parents as a valuable part of our program at Sacramento State. I find that most parents are great boosters and do their part to cheer from the sidelines. On occasion, I hear a comment or witness a behavior from the bleachers that lets me know there was some disagreement with my coaching strategy. Fortunately, I can stay focused on the game and not let it bother me. I learned a long time ago that all the coaches are in the stands!

As a college recruiter, I not only recruit student-athletes, but I recruit the parents as well. Consequently, I spend time with every parent of every prospect we recruit so that parents know what kind of a coach I am, and what kind of a program I run. I have had what other people thought were overbearing parents. But what I learned from those parents is that they just want to be heard. I give them the time, and they are ultimately satisfied. I never have problems.

Sometimes listening to parents and expressing your expectations of them isn't enough. Parents may get too involved, become negative, and ultimately do more harm than good. If they cross that line, you may have to take action.

Find out if your league has guidelines for spectator conduct. If such guidelines exist, make sure every parent gets a copy at the parental meeting before the season begins. If your league doesn't have a policy, the American Sport Education Program has a book entitled *SportParent* that might be helpful. It contains responsibilities and a code of ethics for sports parents. Make your own set of rules and hand out copies.

A national campaign is underway to counter the growing viciousness. The National Alliance for Youth Sports (NAYS) is calling for mandatory sportsmanship training for parents prior to each season. By requiring all parents to attend a sportsmanship clinic, it is believed that peer pressure in the stands can go a long way to keep an otherwise irate parent under control.

COMMUNICATING WITH PARENTS

Keep open lines of communication with parents. Encourage them to talk with you when an issue arises but tell them you will only talk to them out of earshot of the kids when practice or the game is over. Chapter 2 discusses the importance of conducting a parent meeting at the beginning of the season and provides specific topics for discussion. Address rules for parents and make sure they know what is appropriate and inappropriate behavior.

HANDLING PROBLEM PARENTS

Negative parental behavior may never totally be abolished from youth sport, but there are some things you can do. If you have a win-at-all-costs parent, who constantly grumbles about losses and shouts out things like, "C'mon Jane, knock her over if she's in your way next time," or "Hey ref, that's a terrible call. Is the other team paying you off?" talk to the parent privately and remind him or her that it's the effort that counts. Let the parent know that the negative comments and tormenting are harmful to your players and are not welcome.

Stress of Competition

The effect of competitive stress on youth in sports is subject to some debate. Critics of youth sport argue that the stresses of sports participation are bad for kids, while proponents claim sports teach youth to deal with real-life challenges that will provide them with life skills as adults. Competitive stress research shows that anxiety levels for young athletes are generally not higher in competitive sports than those in other childhood activities where performance is inherent.

There are indications, however, that some kids exhibit excessive levels of stress in certain situations. Coaches should be aware of the characteristics of kids who are at risk and prone to excessive stress, and help them to develop strategies for dealing with stressful situations in the sports environment.

In general, stress is viewed as either trait anxiety or state anxiety. Trait anxiety refers to an individual's predisposition to view a situation as threatening or nonthreatening, whereas state anxiety refers to the existing

Coaching Tip

If a parent tries to tell you how to coach, pull the parent aside and tell him or her that opinions should never be voiced in front of the team. The parent may call you at home or talk to you after the game. Coaching strategies are your call, no one else's.

emotional condition of the individual. Athletes feel state anxiety when they get "butterflies" in their stomachs before competition. Trait anxiety and state anxiety are linked, however. A young softball player with high levels of trait anxiety may perceive going up to bat with bases loaded and the tying run on third as a threatening situation. Consequently, she would have high levels of state anxiety. She may feel like her stomach is in a knot, her palms may start to sweat, and muscles may tighten. Another young softball player, with low levels of trait anxiety, may long for the opportunity to bat with the game on the line, because she perceives the situation as nonthreatening. She would, therefore, have lower levels of state anxiety and may go to bat feeling "pumped," focused, and in command of the situation. Athletes vary on whether they perceive situations as threatening or nonthreatening, and, therefore, stress levels will also vary.

There are certain characteristics that coaches can look for in young athletes that may indicate players at risk for excessive levels of competitive stress. Children who exhibit low self-esteem, fear of failure, concerns about being judged by others, and low self-efficacy may be prone to seeing competitive situations as threatening. Coaches can help those athletes by maintaining a positive sport environment and giving constructive feedback.

Just like adults, kids can learn to focus their internal selves on positive outcomes. Use a variety of strategies to help kids cope with the stresses of competition. Relaxation techniques, visualization, and

DEALING WITH STRESS

Routinely spend a few moments talking with your team about stress. In a group setting, ask each player to share an immediate concern or worry. Then tell all of the players that when they come to the softball diamond they should leave all their worries outside the fence the minute they walk onto the field. The softball diamond is a safe place where they can have fun and nothing can hurt them. Give them little strategies to help them deal with stress. If they get scared about something while on the field, tell them to put the worries into their pockets and forget about them. Later, they can empty their pockets into a trash can.

positive self-talk can be taught to young players for use in stressful situations. To teach your players positive self-talk, have them sit in a circle or lie on the grass with their eyes closed. Tell them not to think about red balloons and repeat it over and over. You might say something like, "Don't think about red balloons. Red balloons don't exist." When you have finished, ask them what they were thinking about while you were talking. (Red balloons.) Tell them that that is how positive or negative thoughts work during the games or practice. Ask them to name something negative that could happen during a game (e.g., "Don't strike out."). Have your team close their eyes again and repeat the exercise, substituting the word "strikeout" for "red balloon" (e.g., "I hope I don't strike out."). Ask them what they were thinking about while you were talking. (Striking out.) Now ask them to think of something positive during a game (e.g., "Hit the ball.") and repeat the exercise using a positive statement (e.g., "Think about hitting the ball. Just go up and hit the ball."). Like physical skills, mental skills take practice before they become an acquired skill, so spend part of each practice on positive self-talk.

SEXUAL HARASSMENT

Because most coaches of girls' softball teams are male, the issues of sexual harassment and abuse of power cannot be ignored. Understand what constitutes sexual harassment and learn what is considered appropriate and inappropriate behavior around children. In doing so, you can avoid situations that may leave you vulnerable to accusations of inappropriate behavior.

Athletes of any age want to please their coaches. Young female athletes may be especially vulnerable to adults, who, as coaches, use their power of authority in a situation to violate the trust that is built into the player/coach relationship. In 1998, the Women's Sports Foundation released the following policy regarding romantic or sexual relationships between players and coaches:

> "Romantic and or sexual relationships between coaches and athletes undermine the professionalism of coaches, taint the atmosphere of mutual trust and respect between coach and

athlete, and hinder the fulfillment of the overall educational mission of athletics. The Foundation views it as unethical if coaches engage in romantic and/or sexual relations with athletes under their supervision, even when both parties have apparently consented to the relationship." Hence, it is the coach who will be held accountable if such relationships or conditions exist, because it is generally believed that youth do not have the freedom to remove themselves from such situations.

If you are a male coach, be aware of situations involving players that may leave you vulnerable to accusations of misconduct. Never be alone with a female athlete. If you must address an athlete in private, always have another coach present, preferably a female. It is important to be in group settings with your players and always make sure that there is another adult around.

Refrain from meeting your players alone in social settings. Social activities involving the team are a good idea; however, make parents aware of the event and ask for their help in both coordinating and attending the activity. Don't put yourself in a situation that may be misinterpreted. You don't want to give anyone the idea that you're out on a date.

Physical contact, or touching, between a player and a coach can have serious implications. Some touching in the sport environment is considered appropriate due to the nature of interaction when teaching motor skills. For example, a coach might take the hand of a 7-year-old and position her fingers correctly on a softball to show her the proper grip. Or a coach may help an 8-year-old with hip rota-

AVOIDING POTENTIAL PROBLEMS

If you find yourself in a situation where a female athlete is in need of a ride or she won't be able to attend a team function, try to make arrangements for a parent to transport her. If that doesn't work, have another coach, preferably a female, with you. If it is an emergency situation, call the parent and explain the situation. In addition, call another coach and advise him or her of your intentions. However, do everything you can to avoid these situations.

tion when batting by standing behind her and mechanically turning her hips with his or her hands while she focuses on pivoting on her back foot. There is a big difference between mindful touching in the teaching environment and a coach leaning his or her entire body over and in contact with the back of a 13-year-old repeatedly while showing her the entire swing. In the latter case, the contact is inappropriate. The coach should model the correct movement and the athlete should try to mirror the skill.

Language used by coaches should be closely monitored. Making derogatory comments with sexual overtones, using sexist language, telling dirty jokes, and unwanted touching are all examples of sexual harassment. Other more obvious behaviors include pressuring someone for sex, exhibitionism, fondling, forcible and statutory rape, oral sex, and displaying sexually explicit pictures or written material. According to "The United States Supreme Court and Sexual Harassment Clarification of Issues," in general, any act or actions that are sufficiently severe or pervasive to create a sexually objectionable environment are considered sexual harassment. The best interpretation of sexual harassment with applications to the sports environment that I have seen is the following excerpt by Susan Strauss in *Sexual Harassment and Teens:*

> Sexual harassment becomes illegal:
>
> 1. When the harassment is made a condition of employ-
>   ment or situation. A person cannot hire or fire another
>   person based on whether or not she goes along with
>   his/her sexual advances. This type of advance can be
>   explicit (clearly stated) or implicit (understood but not
>   directly stated). This can be applied in sports settings
>   where a coach approaches a player sexually by saying
>   she must go along with what the coach wants or she
>   won't make the team or get a starting position.
>
> 2. When the activity or language provides an uncomfort-
>   able work setting or learning environment. This tends
>   to be the most common type of sexual harassment
>   found in the school. It can come from a teammate who
>   is bigger than another player or has more friends or
>   social status or an adult coach. When a person feels

intimidated or offended, . . ., she may be in a sexually harassing environment. Many factors go into determining whether the behavior by another is considered sexual harassment. These factors include who the person is, what the relationship is with that person, whether that person has power over the other and the time and place of the incident.

As a coach, you must understand sexual harassment. It is your responsibility to make sure that the sports environment you provide for your athletes is free of the conditions considered harassment. Realize that your position of authority as a coach is centered on a relationship with your athletes that is built on trust. Once you cross a line sexually with an athlete, you have violated that trust. Accusations of abuse and sexual harassment are career-ending, and you may likely carry that stigma for the rest of your life.

Girls experience tremendous change throughout childhood. These changes, combined with social pressures, can make the transition from childhood to adolescence difficult. You must understand the special needs of your athletes and the implications of this transition on their sports experience. Be aware of the manifestations of competitive stress, eating disorders, and other issues that may have serious consequences for you and your players. By being forewarned, you can be forearmed. Pay attention and get involved!

SOFTBALL BASICS

I'LL BET EVERY coach dreams of someday winning the championship. It's not hard to envision the final play of the game, that last out on a ground ball to the shortstop. And then the team erupts in jubilation. There you are, being carried off the field on the shoulders of your players amidst wild cheering and chants of, "We're number one!" Before you pop the champagne cork, realize that the road to the championship has a beginning, and somewhere in the beginning there are the basics.

Softball basics lay a solid foundation of knowledge for your athletes. In addition to fundamental skills, you'll want to know about softball equipment so that you can advise your players and their parents on what they should buy. Picking out the right bat and glove can be confusing. It's important to have the right team equipment so that your team is properly prepared. The right equipment can enhance performance and reduce the risk of injury.

In addition to equipment, take the time to learn the basics of position play on the field. Understand primary and secondary responsibilities of each position and how they work together. The more you know, the more you can teach your team so they'll have better command of the game. As a result, the experience will be more enjoyable for everyone.

One of the most important decisions you will make as a coach is selecting a staff. Every coach needs a supporting cast. The personnel you select to assist you with the team should be chosen with care. Evaluate your needs and choose individuals accordingly. When you have the right people, your job will be much easier, and you will be rewarded many times over.

Finally, learn all the rules of the game. This is easily one of the most overlooked parts of coaching. It always seems like there is so much to do that somehow, finding time to read the rulebook becomes a huge chore. After all, how complicated can the rules be? Take time to find out. It's not unusual to find that on occasion, you may be able to use a rule to reverse an umpire's call.

EQUIPMENT

Properly equip your team so that your athletes can be effective. Equipment can be broken down into team equipment and personal equipment. Personal equipment, which will likely be purchased by the individual players on your team, consists of a bat, glove, and cleats. Some kids may want to purchase their own batting helmets, and that's okay. Even if some kids have their own helmets, however, batting helmets should definitely be included with team equipment. Other team equipment includes catcher's gear, balls, and bats. Although your practice and playing fields will probably have bases,

PITCHER'S GEAR

You may find it helpful to include a stake down pitching rubber, hammer, and tape measure in the bag containing the catcher's gear. By keeping these items with the pitcher's gear, you'll always have them around. When your pitcher warms up on the sidelines before a game, use the tape measure to mark off the correct pitching distance, and use the hammer to stake down the pitcher's rubber. You can then use the home plate from the set of throw-down bases that you keep in the bag as well. When your pitcher warms up for the game, she'll be able to establish the proper game feel of the mound by warming up on one.

you may want to invest in an inex-
pensive set of throw-down thin rubber bases for the times you need a
set. These bases can be easily carried
in the bag with the catcher's gear.
You'll be surprised at how often they
come in handy.

Invest in additional team equipment for teaching and training your
players. These items include batting
tees, pitching machines with poly-ure-
thane balls for batting practice, and
nets for batters to hit into. Although
these items will not be addressed here,
sporting goods stores specializing in
baseball and softball equipment will be able to assist you further.

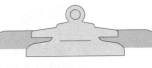

Coaching Tip

Check with your league on
what equipment they supply
and what athletes must provide. Make this information
available to parents at your
first team meeting. Check
the rulebook annually for
equipment specifications.

Personal items that each player should own include shoes or
cleats, a fielder's glove, and a bat. Cleats and gloves fit individuals
differently, and gloves have a certain "feel" when using them. In
addition, cleats and gloves get "broken in" and tend to form-fit the
performer's foot or hand. For this reason, provide guidance on how
to choose these items yet require that the participants purchase them
themselves. Because bats are so expensive, you may want to provide
some team bats should players wish to use the team's assortment
rather than their own.

Shoes

Softball/baseball shoes, or cleats, are personal in nature and should
be purchased by the athletes. Soccer cleats are similar to softball
cleats except that they don't have a toe cleat, which helps a runner
lead off base. Shoes that have soles with soft rubber cleats are legal
for youth play. Metal cleats, hard rubber cleats, and detachable cleats
that screw on are all illegal for youth play. Shoes with flat bottoms
make for slippery footing on both the infield dirt and outfield grass
and should be avoided.

Gloves

Softball/baseball gloves should be chosen with great care. They come in different sizes, colors, and grades of leather. (Don't buy a vinyl glove. They wear out quickly and don't break in well.) Although stiff at first, gloves will "break in" and soften with play (glove oil may expedite the break-in process). In general, the more expensive the glove, the higher the grade of leather.

Defensive players wear fielder's gloves or mitts. Fielder's *gloves* have defined fingers and an area, called the "pocket," where the ball is caught. *Mitts* also have a pocket, but they differ from a glove in that they have an undefined finger section, much like a mitten. Softball mitts are legal only for catchers and first basemen. Beginning players should select smaller gloves that are lighter in weight. The glove should not be too tight or too loose on the hand. Ultimately, the player should choose a glove that is easy to control.

Gloves come in a variety of colors, and you may suggest to your players that they select tan, brown, or black glove colors. According to softball rules that govern most play, gloves may not be the color of the ball but may be any combination of other colors. The pitcher's glove must be one solid color other than white, gray, or optic yellow. Gloves with white, gray, or optic yellow circles on the outside are illegal for all players because they give the appearance of a ball. Since some kids play more than one position and may also pitch, solid colors of tan, brown, or black would be the sensible choice.

Bats

Alloy bats come in varying sizes and colors. Standard bat lengths for young girls range from 27 to 32 inches. The weight also varies according to length and will be generally referred to as "drop." A 27-inch bat may have an 8-ounce drop (−8), which means it weighs 19 ounces. Subtract the number referred to as the "ounce drop" from the bat length to arrive at the bat weight. A 32-inch bat with a 10-ounce drop will weigh 22 ounces.

Ideally, hitters want good bat speed and bat control. A bat that is too heavy won't hit the ball farther if the batter can't bring it around in time to hit the pitch. There are several tests to use to determine the best fit for weight and length. The best way to test a bat for proper weight is to have the player hold the bat at the base of the grip with one hand. Standing with feet together, have the player hold the bat straight out to the side with one arm (see figure 4.1). If the bat is too heavy, she will struggle to keep it on a vertical plane. She should be able to keep it steady.

The proper length can also be determined by another simple test. While standing with feet together, set the end of the bat on the ground at the player's side with the knob at the hip (see figure 4.2). Place the palm of the hand on that side of the body directly on the knob. If the arm is slightly bent at the elbow, you have what should be a good fit for length.

Make sure the bat meets ASA performance standards. Beginning in 2000, all bats must have an ASA-approved stamp or be included on a list of approved bat models published by the ASA National

FIGURE 4.1
Bat test to determine proper weight.

FIGURE 4.2
Bat test to determine proper length.

Office. Bats manufactured prior to 1995 are legal if, at the sole discretion of the umpire, they were in compliance with the ASA performance standards that were in effect at that time.

Batting Helmets

All players on offense (e.g., batter, baserunners, and on-deck batter in the circle) must wear a double earflap protective helmet approved by the National Operating Committee on Standards for Athletic Equipment (NOCSAE). All helmets must be the same color, and the NOCSAE stamp and exterior warning label must be visible.

Catcher's Gear

All catchers must wear protective gear. Protective gear consists of a facemask with a throat protector, a helmet with earflaps, chest protector, and leg guards. Most facemasks come with a built-in throat protector. Make sure proper fit is established with catching gear. The helmet and facemask should fit snuggly and should not shift around with the catcher's movements. Leg guards should protect the legs from the foot to the kneecaps, and the chest protector should be snug but not tight, and never sagging or drooping. In youth play, any player warming up a pitcher must wear a mask with a throat protector and a helmet with earflaps.

Balls

Softballs come in different sizes, colors, and degrees of hardness. A 12-inch softball is used in adult play ($11^7/_8$ to $12^1/_8$ inches in maximum circumference) and weighs no more than 7 ounces. Youth leagues use 10- and 11-inch balls, with lighter weights depending upon the age group. Check with your league to find out which ball you should use.

White balls with white stitching appear to be going the way of the dinosaur. More and more leagues (both slow- and fast-pitch) are changing to the optic yellow ball with red stitching. Again, check with your league to see which ball has been adopted for play in your area.

THE LIFE OF A BAT

Did you know that bats have a life expectancy? There is only so much "pop" in an aluminum bat. After a lot of use, the walls of the bat lose their resiliency, and the rebound effect of the ball off of the bat diminishes. How long a bat lasts depends on a number of things. Taking good care of the bat when transporting it and never throwing the bat will help prolong its life. Other factors are the number of balls hit and the kind of balls hit. Hard polyurethane balls commonly used in pitching machines are hard on bats and can "deaden" a bat very quickly. If you use a machine with polyurethane balls, it is a good idea to have older team bats that everyone can use for batting practice. Players can save their own bats for game use.

Softballs also vary in degrees of hardness. The cover generally is smooth and consists of chrome-tanned horsehide, cowhide, or other approved synthetic material. Its seams are stitched with cotton or linen thread and raised for grip and trajectory. The core is made of a polyurethane mixture, kapok, or a mixture of cork and rubber. Core centers have different degrees of hardness and are noted by the coefficient of restitution (COR). Harder cores cause the ball to have greater rebound ability off the bat, which causes the ball to travel faster and farther when struck. Softer cores with lower CORs are used in youth play.

POSITION PLAY

Position play in the sport of softball refers to individual responsibilities of specific players at their positions on defense. For the team to function together effectively on defense, it is important that players understand their roles and responsibilities at each position. Defensively, the softball diamond is divided into to an infield and an outfield. The infield is the dirt area that encompasses the pitcher's mound, home plate, and all three bases. Players who take positions on the dirt are referred to as infielders. The outfield is the grassy area from the edge of the infield dirt to the outfield fence. Players who play on the grass are referred to as outfielders.

Each fielder has primary and secondary responsibilities. Primary responsibilities are actions taken to make a play and usually involve the ball and a batter/runner. For example, the primary responsibility of the first baseman is to cover first base on a ground ball hit on the infield. Secondary responsibilities are actions away from the play whereby a player stands by ready to assist, as is often the situation with backing up a base in case of an overthrow.

Figure 4.3 shows the nine defensive starting positions and each player's respective coverage area. It is each player's primary responsibility to field balls that enter their coverage areas. Coverage areas don't have specific boundaries, and the coverage areas may vary slightly depending upon the speed and ability of your players, but in general, these areas are assigned to certain positions. Without boundary lines, communication with teammates on the perimeters is critical.

Infield position players have responsibilities to cover certain bases. They may be called upon to cover their own base or cover the base of a teammate who has left her base open to go field the ball. Very young softball players will probably not understand the concept of when to cover a teammate's base, so you may want to keep it very simple by having them focus on just their own base in the beginning. As they grow older and understand their own positions, you can begin to add other base coverages. Figure 4.4 shows the infield positions and their respective base coverage responsibilities.

Rules of right-of-way apply on the softball diamond to different positions. Balls are often hit into the air between fielders, and more than one player could make the catch. It is important to establish who has priority over other fielders on the play, or who has right-of-way to the ball, so that fielders can avoid collisions when trying to catch the ball. Whenever a ball is hit in the air between two or more fielders, each player should run hard after the ball. The instant that a

SOFTBALLS

The optic yellow softball with red stitching made its first appearance in all divisions of women's NCAA softball for the 1992-93 season. This new ball was designed with the intent of providing hitters with improved visibility. It is believed that the red-stitched seams are easier to see against an optic yellow cover than the old ball with white stitches on a white cover. In theory, hitters should be able to see seam rotation better, which should improve hitting. Studies to date have been inconclusive as to whether the optic yellow ball has enhanced a batter's visibility in hitting a softball.

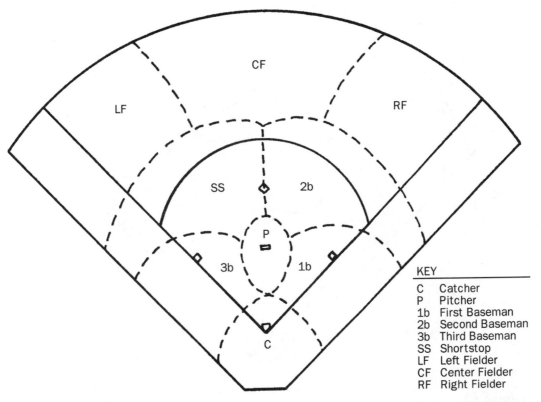

FIGURE 4.3
Starting positions of all nine defensive players and their coverage areas.

fielder feels she can make the catch, she should yell out, "ball," or, "mine," and continue calling. The adjacent fielders also on the run should acknowledge her call by yelling, "take it," or, "yours." Other players who are nearby but not involved in the play should help by calling the name of the player who is calling the ball (e.g., "Nancy! Nancy!"). If two or more fielders call for the ball at the same time, then the right-of-way rules apply and that player who has priority should make the catch. Figure 4.5 shows the starting defensive positions and who has priority over other fielders. In general, you should note that:

1. Outfielders have priority over infielders.
2. The center fielder has priority over both the right and left fielders.

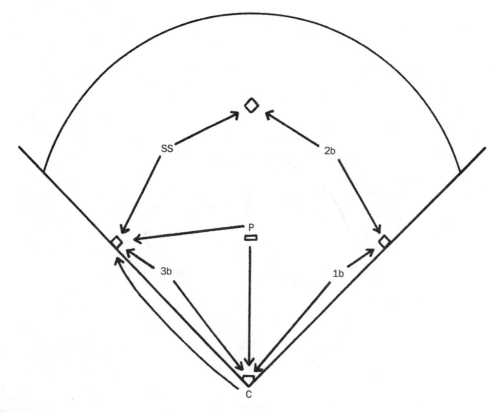

FIGURE 4.4
Starting positions of all infielders and their base coverage responsibilities.

3. All infielders have priority over the catcher.
4. The shortstop has priority over most of the infielders.
5. All infielders have priority over the pitcher except the catcher.

All defensive positions have secondary responsibilities. Secondary responsibilities consist of things like backing up a base for a possible overthrow or backing up a teammate in the act of fielding a ball. Teach your fielders to make the back-up play as if they are expecting the overthrow or the miss. Too many players go through the motions with secondary responsibilities, assuming their duties won't be needed, only to get caught by surprise when they really are needed. Make sure your outfielders stay back far enough when backing up a throw on the infield. They may have a tendency to creep in and get too close to the play. Table 4.1 summarizes the defensive positions, showing their primary and secondary responsibilities.

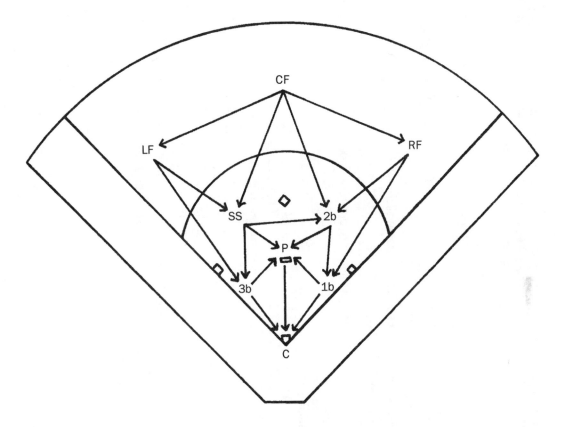

FIGURE 4.5
Starting defensive positions and rules of right-of-way. Arrows show which players have priority or right-of-way over other fielders.

All of the fielders have a number that corresponds to the position they play on defense. These numbers (see figure 4.6) refer to locations on the softball diamond and are used in scoring a game. For example, if a right-handed batter tends to pull the ball a lot and I want to move the shortstop closer to third base to defend the 5-6 hole, I am referring to the area on the field that exists between the third baseman (5) and the shortstop (6). The term "hole" merely refers to the hitting lane between two defensive players on the field. When scoring a game, record the play where the shortstop fields a ground ball and throws to first for the out as 6-3. If the right fielder makes the catch on a fly ball, record F-9. Your rulebook should have information regarding how to score a game.

Table 4.1   A summary of the primary and secondary responsibilities of position players on defense.

POSITION	PRIMARY RESPONSIBILITIES	SECONDARY RESPONSIBILITIES
Pitcher	Field balls in coverage area	Back up home on all throws from outfield with runner in scoring position
	Cover home on wild pitch (optional*)	Back up third base on fly ball to right with runner on second base
	Cover third base on bunt if 3b fields the ball with a runner on first base (hold until catcher arrives)	Back up second on all throws from outfield
Catcher	Field balls in coverage area	Back up first base on infield ground balls (with no runners on)
	Cover home	
	Cover third base on bunt with runner at first when 3b fields ball (replace pitcher on coverage)	
First Baseman	Field balls in coverage area	Back up second base on throws from LF
	Receive throws to first base	
	Cover home on wild pitch	
Second Baseman	Field balls in coverage area	Back up balls hit to 1b
	Receive throws to second base from 3b, SS, RF	Back up throw by catcher to pitcher with runner on 2b
	Cover first base on a bunt	Back up second base on LF throw to SS
	Cover first base when 1b fields ball	
	Relay home throws from RF	

POSITION	PRIMARY RESPONSIBILITIES	SECONDARY RESPONSIBILITIES
Third Baseman	Field balls in coverage area Receive throws to 3b Cover home on wild pitch (optional*)	Back up RF throw to second base
Shortstop	Field balls in coverage area Receive throws at second base on steal, on double play from P, C, 1b, 2b Receive outfield throws at second base from LF, CF Relay home outfield throws from LF, CF Cover third base on steal from 2b Take throws at third base when 3b fields ball	Back up balls hit to 3b Back up balls hit to P
Left Fielder	Field balls in coverage area Back up all balls thrown to third base Back up balls thrown to second base from 1b, 2b, RF	Back up balls hit to CF, SS, 3b
Center Fielder	Field balls in coverage area Back up balls hit to 2b, SS Back up balls thrown to second base from P, C, 1b, 3b	Back up balls hit to RF, LF
Right Fielder	Field balls in coverage area Back up balls thrown to first base Back up balls thrown to second base from SS, 3b	Back up balls hit to CF, 2b, 1b

* Optional coverages with the pitcher and 3b covering home on a wild pitch have to do with the coach's preference. In general, keep your pitcher out of the coverage if possible (to avoid injury at the plate). It is, however, usually the pitcher who first knows that the ball is way off target and will be first to react and theoretically can get there fastest. To avoid injury to the pitcher, assign the responsibility to the first baseman primarily. The third baseman should also charge and the first baseman and third baseman should work together to get the plate covered.

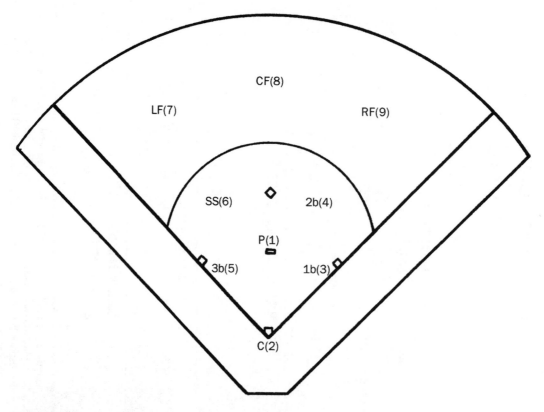

FIGURE 4.6
Defensive players showing corresponding numbers for the positions.

CHOOSING A SUPPORT STAFF

Choosing a support staff is one of the most important things you do as a coach. Your staff will include several assistant coaches and a manager who can double as a scorekeeper during games. Carefully evaluate your needs and your situation before you solicit assistance. These individuals are an extension of you, and you want to be sure they fit well with your program.

Young girls need female role models in positions of leadership. In addition, young girls will have specific needs and concerns at times, and will likely feel more comfortable talking with a female coach. Therefore, it is important that a girls' softball team have female representation on the coaching staff. Whether the female coach is the head coach or an assistant coach is not important. Biological changes and the onset of puberty are just a few examples of times when a female coach will be beneficial, if not advantageous for the situation.

In looking for assistant coaches, honestly evaluate yourself as a head coach. What are your strengths? What are your weaknesses? Do you know anything about pitching? Are you comfortable working with hitting? The answers to these questions will help you develop a coaching profile of your-

Coaching Tip

Outfielders are the last lines of defense, so practice over-throws on the infield to help outfielders gauge how far back they should be to contain the ball.

self first. This profile will help you determine what kind of staff you are likely to need. Once you have identified your weaknesses, then you are ready to begin your search for assistance. Find people who have knowledge of the game and expertise in the areas that you do not. If, for example, you don't know much about pitching in fast-pitch softball, find someone who does. Pitching is a core part of the game, and you need someone with the knowledge and expertise to develop and work with the pitching staff. You may find that some of your pitchers already have pitching coaches that they see several times a week, and that's okay. Only you can decide if you know enough to guide your pitchers effectively through practices and games.

In your search for coaches, keep in mind a few intangibles that determine whether an individual will be a good fit for your program. An individual's character should be of great importance to you. Remember that this person will be in a position of authority and will be working with children. Ask yourself whether the individual you are considering would be a good role model. Would the person be a positive teacher? Would he or she be willing to make the time commitment involved in coaching? And what about loyalty? Assistant coaches who undermine head coaches with negative talk and backstabbing are dangerous people. Do a little homework in the beginning and conduct interviews with candidates. Time well spent at this juncture will save you heartache and help you considerably down the road.

Assigning responsibilities to your coaching staff will help things run more smoothly. You may decide to have a coach who works with infielders and a coach who works with outfielders. In preparing your team for games, assign each coach specific pre-game duties to prepare for competition. For example, your outfield coach can hit fly balls to your outfielders prior to a game, and your infield coach can hit grounders to your infielders. Then, when it's time to take pre-game infield, one coach can be assigned to hit pre-game and do it on a consistent basis. This will keep things organized and eliminate confusion.

A good manager is invaluable to your staff and often is the glue that keeps everything together. You may find a parent of a player or spouse of a coach who can be at every game and practice. Good organizational skills and the desire to help are key ingredients. The manager should be able to keep the score book during games and assist you in organizing the team for games, practices, and various other functions.

THE GAME

In November 1887, softball was invented in Chicago, Illinois, inside the Farragut Boat Club. Alumni from Harvard and Yale were convened at the club and were anxiously awaiting the score of the Harvard-Yale football game played that day. When it was announced that Yale had defeated Harvard 17-8, a zealous Yale fan picked up an old boxing glove and threw it at a Harvard supporter who tried to hit the glove back with a stick. George Hancock, a reporter for the Chicago Board of Trade, witnessed the event and suggested an indoor game of baseball. Hancock took a piece of chalk and marked off a home plate, bases, and a pitcher's box inside the Farragut Club gym, and the first game of softball, or indoor-outdoor as it was called then, was played.

The sport gained in popularity and eventually spread to Minneapolis and a fire department lieutenant named Louis Rober. In January 2000, the ASA reported on its Web site (www.softball.org) that Lieutenant Rober wanted to keep his firemen fit during their idle time, so he used a vacant lot adjacent to the fire station and laid out a diamond. He used a small medicine ball and a bat that was 2 inches in diameter and began playing. Soon other fire departments were playing the game and in 1895, Rober transferred to another company and taught the game to his new crew. He subsequently put together a team and called them the Kittens. Indoor-outdoor soon became known as Kitten Ball. In 1925, the Minneapolis Park Board changed the name of the game to Diamond Ball. Finally, in 1926, Walter Hakanson, a YMCA official from Denver, suggested the game be called softball, and the name remains today.

Today, softball is played all over the world in various forms. The game is basically either fast-pitch or slow-pitch, with modifications for different levels of play. For example, the pitching distance in men's fast-pitch is 46 feet, the collegiate game is 43 feet, and some levels of youth play is 35 feet. While bunting and stealing is not allowed with beginners, it is allowed in more advanced levels of fast-pitch play.

HOME VS. AWAY

A regulation game consists of seven innings with the visiting team batting first and the home team batting last. If playing at a neutral site, the home team and visitors are decided by a coin toss. If the home team is ahead after $6^1/_2$ innings of play, then the game is declared over and the home team does not bat in the bottom half of the 7th inning. This would also be the case if, in the bottom half of the 7th inning, the home team goes ahead to take the lead. The game is declared over when the go ahead run is scored, and the home team is declared the winner.

Rules of the Game

Although there are different leagues and organizations with various rules, specific consideration in this book was given to the ASA rules that govern play. Always consult your own rulebook and league for modifications of the rules adapted for your level of play. Rules change, so keep abreast of new developments.

Two teams of nine or more players play the game of softball. All nine defensive players are on the field at once playing defense, while the offensive team sends a batter to home plate one player at a time. The pitcher on defense uses an underhand motion to throw a ball to a batter who attempts to hit the ball with a bat. The batter tries to hit the ball so that the defense can't get to it in time to put the batter out. Each member of the offensive team must take an "at bat," starting at home plate, and either hit the ball or draw a walk to advance to first base and beyond in an attempt to score a run. A run is scored when a batter becomes a baserunner and legally touches the bases in the correct order before finally touching home plate to end her turn on offense.

The defensive team consists of nine players in a defensive alignment on the field of play. The defense attempts to get three outs before a runner on offense can score a run. An out is when a runner does not reach base safely. Each team takes a turn on offense and defense, which, together, constitute an inning. There are six outs in an inning (three outs made by each team while on defense). The team scoring the most runs after seven innings of play is declared the winner.

Field of Play

The layout of a softball field is depicted in figure 4.7. The playing field consists of fair territory and foul territory. Fair territory is that area on the ground and in the air between the foul lines and inside the outfield fence. Foul territory is that area between the foul lines (first and third baselines and left and right field lines) and out-of-play or dead ball territory. Play is halted on any ball that goes into an out-of-play or dead ball area. Softball fields have an infield area that is dirt, and an outfield area that is grassy. Modifications for different levels of play will likely affect the following distances: pitch-

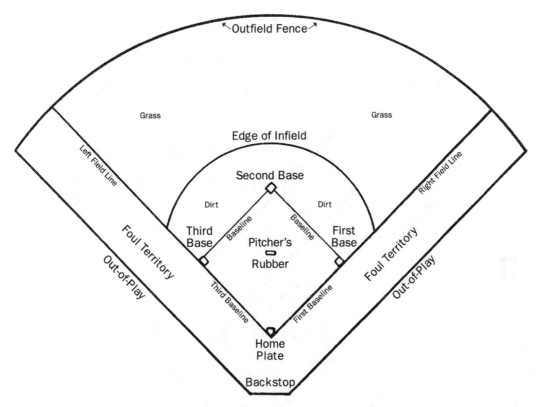

FIGURE 4.7
Layout of an official softball field.

ing distance, distances between bases, and distance from home plate to the outfield fence. Figure 4.8 and table 4.2 show how distances are measured and includes measurements for an official softball field.

Players and Substitutes

To begin and continue a fast-pitch softball game, each team must have nine people present in the dugout or field area. (The "short-handed rule," effective in 1999, however, allows the game to begin with eight players in fast-pitch only. See your rulebook for further details.) The nine players occupy the positions of pitcher, catcher, first base, second base, third base, shortstop, left field, center field, and right field. Note that defensive players may change positions at

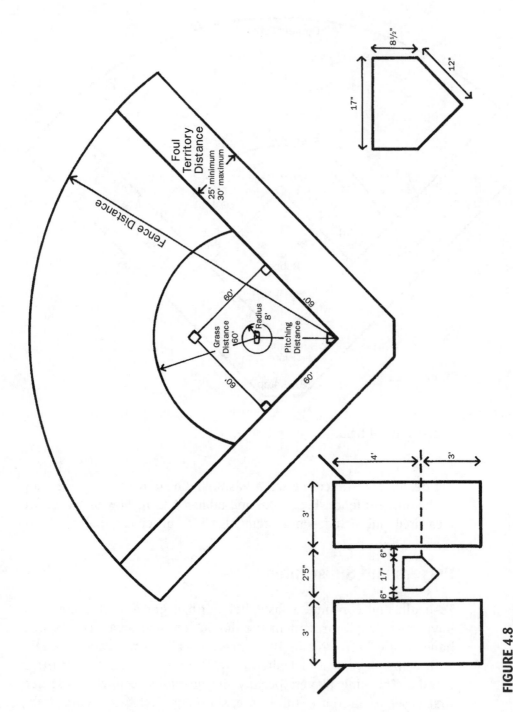

FIGURE 4.8
Official softball field and how distances are measured.

Table 4.2	Youth Fast-Pitch Official Distance Table			
Division	**Bases**	**Pitching**	**Minimum Fence**	**Maximum Fence**
Girls 10U	60'	35'	150'	175'
Girls 12U	60'	40'	175'	200'
Girls 14U	60'	40'	175'	200'

any time as long as the umpire is notified. Defensive players may also be substituted for at any time.

Each team takes its turn on offense by sending hitters (batters) to home plate to bat in a specified batting order. A batter becomes a baserunner by hitting the ball in fair territory without causing an out to be made directly on her by the defense. Batters may not change positions in the batting order, but they may be substituted for at any time. A designated player (DP) may be used to hit for any defensive player and must be listed in the batting order. The DP must remain in the same position in the batting order for the entire game. The player for whom the DP is batting shall play defense only (DEFO) and shall be listed in the tenth spot on the line-up card.

Any player on defense or offense may be substituted for at any time. The umpire must be notified of any substitution. A starting player may be substituted for and re-enter the game one time. Once a starter leaves and then re-enters the game, she must leave the game permanently if substituted for again. A substitute may enter the game only one time. She may not leave the game and re-enter. Courtesy runners may run for the pitcher and/or catcher in youth ball only. Check your rulebook for details regarding courtesy runners.

Pitching

The pitch is the action used by the defense to put the ball in play. A legal pitch must be used to deliver the ball to the batter for either a ball or a strike. If the pitcher throws four balls to the batter, the batter is awarded first base. If the pitcher throws three strikes to the batter, then the batter is out, and if it is the third out of the inning, then both teams switch sides. If it is not the third out of the inning, then the next batter takes her turn at the plate for an at bat.

A pitch is declared a strike by the umpire when the pitcher uses a legal underhand motion to deliver the ball so that it passes through the batter's strike zone, or when a pitch is swung on and is either missed or fouled off out of play. If, on the third strike, the batter fouls off a pitch, she continues to bat regardless of the number of foul balls she may hit. A batter's strike zone will be modified with different levels of play; however, it is generally that area over the plate between the batter's shoulders and knees. If the ball does not pass through this zone, then the umpire calls the pitch a ball.

An official softball field requires an eight-foot circle around the pitcher's rubber. This circle specifically applies to baserunners. When the pitcher has possession of the ball within the circle, the baserunner(s) not in contact with a base must immediately commit to advancing to the next base or returning to the base previously touched.

Batting

Each member of the offensive team must take her turn at bat according to the batting order. She must take a position inside the batter's box and attempt to hit the ball or draw a walk during her at bat. After three strikes are declared (except for a foul ball on the last pitch), the batter is out. If the batter receives four balls from the pitcher before having three strikes against her, she is awarded first base and becomes a baserunner.

When a batter hits the ball with the bat, the ball is considered either fair or foul. A fair ball is a batted ball that is directly hit into fair territory between first base and third base that either settles on the ground fair or is first touched while fair. A foul ball is a batted ball that is directly hit into foul territory outside of the foul lines that settles there or is first touched while foul. A batter may attempt to reach first base safely on a batted ball that is considered fair, and may advance on the base paths legally until she is declared out or crosses home plate and scores a run. A foul ball is called a strike on the batter (except if it is the third strike). A batter may not end her at bat on a foul ball.

Baserunning

A batter becomes a baserunner after she hits the ball fair and attempts to reach base. She may score a run by touching the bases legally in the correct order and reaching home without being put out or before the third out in the inning (unless the third out is a force play, see below). If a baserunner needs to return to a base, she must touch the bases in reverse order. A baserunner may overrun first base *only,* without liability to be put out. If she overruns any other bases (except home plate), she is liable to be put out.

Baserunners are primarily out by being tagged or forced out. A tag out is when a runner is touched with the ball while in between bases while the ball is in the possession of a defensive player. A force out occurs when a runner, who is being forced to advance to the next base because of a preceding runner, is either tagged with the ball while advancing or put out with the ball arriving at the base in a defensive player's possession, ahead of the runner. There are many other ways a baserunner can be out. Read the rulebook for further clarification.

If you're going to make the time to coach, be the best you can be! Take the time to learn softball basics and work to develop a team that is fundamentally sound. Select a coaching staff that will be complementary to you and that will provide you with something different from what you already know. Work hard to provide your coaches with the same consideration you expect of them. In addition, educate yourself and be in a position to guide and advise your athletes and their parents on the selection and purchase of equipment. Learn the rules and know what the rules say about softball equipment. If you lay a strong foundation for your team with the basics, your players will grow with knowledge and experience more enjoyment out of playing the game. And who knows, you may not win the championship, but there's always time to celebrate a job that's well done!

5

THE HOW-TO'S OF
INDIVIDUAL DEFENSIVE PLAY

ALTHOUGH SOFTBALL IS a team sport, sound individual play is a prerequisite to solid team play on defense. Each player must know how to execute basic defensive skills and understand strategies to play a defensive position. Your shortstop, for example, must be able to field a ground ball and throw to first base accurately. It is also her responsibility to cover second base on a steal. Work with her on her fielding skills and drill her with the infielders on base coverage in practice.

The most basic skills of individual defensive play are throwing, catching, and fielding. Without them, it is impossible to play softball or to make outs on defense. The object of the offensive team is to hit the ball so that the defense can't make outs, and it is the object of the defensive team to field the ball as quickly as possible to make outs.

Two of the most specialized skills in fast-pitch softball are pitching and catching. Together, these positions are referred to as the battery. The two positions essentially work together to try to stop hitters from reaching base. Good pitchers can be somewhat effective by themselves, but good catchers can make average pitchers look phenomenal.

In this chapter, you'll learn the specifics of individual defensive play. The skills are broken down into their components, and drills are provided to help you develop young players. Above all, practice and repetition of the skills will be necessary for improvement. Keep your teaching simple, and structure your practice opportunities for your athletes' success. When they succeed, they feel a sense of accomplishment and increased self-confidence. This can be an empowering experience that will keep them coming back for more!

HOW TO THROW

Throwing a softball means getting the ball from point A to point B as directly as possible. There are a number of different ways to throw. Players may throw overhand or underhand. Outfielders use overhand throwing with an added crow-hop (see page 98), which helps them with the longer throws that they have to make. Infielders use variations in overhand throwing, which generally consist of throws designed to get rid of the ball quicker. Side-arm throwing, for example, is used by the shortstop to begin the double play. The second baseman frequently uses the side-arm throw to throw to first base. Another variation of the overhand throw is the quick-snap throw, commonly used by infielders in run-downs. Underhand throws, consisting of forehand and backhand flips or tosses, are used by infielders for the shortest distances on the field.

The Grip

For just about all throws, the ball should be held in the fingers and not pressed into the palm of the hand. The three middle fingers should be spread out evenly on one side of the ball with the soft fleshy pads of the fingertips on a seam. The little finger should fit comfortably alongside the ball for stability, and the thumb should take a position on the ball that is in opposition to the three middle fingers (see figure 5.1). Gripping the ball on a seam helps prevent slippage on release and helps with trajectory on the throw.

To test for correct ball position in the fingers and not the palm, check the following: With the ball properly seated in the throwing hand of a player, tell the player to take the four fingers of her non-throwing hand, minus the thumb, and lay them along the palm of the

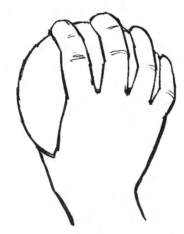

FIGURE 5.1
The softball grip.

throwing hand. How far up the palm do her fingers go? When her fingers reach a depth that places the middle knuckles at the heel of her throwing hand, then the ball is properly positioned in the fingers on the grip.

An infielder's grip on the ball is slightly firmer, or tighter, than an outfielder's grip. You should be able to easily pull the ball out of the hand of an outfielder who is using the proper tension in her grip. If you try to pull the ball out of the grip of an infielder, you should meet with mild resistance due to the amount of tension in the grip. Whenever playing conditions are such that the ball is wet (e.g., rain), all fielders should loosen their grips slightly so that the ball doesn't spurt out of the hand and misfire to any degree upon release to throw.

The next sections describe the proper mechanics for throwing. All descriptions assume a right-handed thrower. References made to "right" and "left" should be switched for a left-handed thrower.

The Overhand Throw

The basic overhand throwing pattern consists of the windup, the throw, and the follow-through. The windup places the body in the correct position to begin the actual throw, or to execute the mechanics of effectively launching the ball at the intended target. The follow-through dissipates all the forces generated by the body during the throw to reduce the risk of injury to the body. Thus, if all parts of the overhand throw aren't executed properly, the athlete may struggle with consistent performance, and arm injuries are likely to result.

The Windup

The windup is a series of movements designed to put the body in the best position to throw the ball. To begin the windup, the player stands with both hands together chest-high, facing the intended target. She then shifts her weight onto her left leg and steps toward the target with the right leg. As she steps, she points her right foot outward so that she can rotate her body to the right so her left side faces the target. As her body rotates right, her hands separate and move in opposite directions. The glove hand points at the target with the arm extended. The throwing hand traverses a downward arc past the right hip and to a position behind the body and above the shoulder with the elbow bent at a 90-degree angle. The ball is facing opposite the target. As the hands separate to these positions, the left leg is lifted forward off the ground with the knee bent slightly. This completes the windup phase and prepares the body for the throw.

The Throw

The athlete begins with all of her weight on her right leg while the left leg is up in the air with the knee bent in preparation to step. As she steps toward the target with the left leg, the shoulders and trunk rotate around to the left, simultaneously bringing the throwing shoulder forward while the glove hand drops to a position along the left hip with the elbow bent. The right elbow leads the throwing arm forward with the upper arm perpendicular to the ground and the hand behind and slightly under the ball so that the wrist is cocked. All of the athlete's weight is transferred onto the front foot. The hand and wrist snap through the ball to complete the throwing phase.

The Follow-Through

After the player releases the ball, her weight is forward on the left foot. The throwing arm becomes relaxed, and the hand continues on a path across the front of the body, ending at the opposite hip. The athlete bends forward at the waist and slightly bends the left knee. The right leg comes up off the ground and bends slightly. Upon completion of the throw, the fielder momentarily remains balanced on the front leg before stepping down with the right leg to fully ground her body. For a look at all steps of the overhand throw, see figure 5.2.

FIGURE 5.2
The overhand throw.

Quick-snap and side-arm throws are two variations of overhand throwing. They are generally used by infielders when there is little time and the distance is short. Underhand throws that consist of short tosses or flips are also used by infielders when quick plays are needed and the intended target is within 6 to 8 feet.

Quick-Snap Throw

The quick-snap throw is executed with the elbow, forearm, wrist, and fingers of the throwing hand. The athlete stands facing the target with her hands together at chest level and her feet approximately hip-width apart. The throw begins by shifting the weight onto the right foot while stepping with the left foot toward the target. Simultaneously, the hands separate and the glove arm extends with the glove pointing at the target. The right hand is taken up over the shoulder with the arm bent at a 90-degree angle, allowing the elbow to face out (upper arm parallel to the ground) and placing the ball at a position even with the right ear. The throw is made with the right elbow leading the ball forward, followed by a pronounced snap of the wrist and roll of the fingers forward under the ball. The glove hand drops to a comfortable position at the left hip with the elbow bent. (See figure 5.3.)

FIGURE 5.3
The quick-snap throw.

Side-Arm Throw

The side-arm throw is executed by an infielder in her fielding position. The key is to get the athlete to stay low to the ground. After fielding a ground ball, the player keeps her knees and waist bent and rotates her trunk around to the right, taking both hands back to her throwing shoulder. Her right elbow is bent and extended out to the rear. The upper arm is parallel to the ground. She then steps with her left foot toward the target and pulls her glove arm out, pointing the glove at the target. The elbow leads the throwing arm forward to begin the throw. The glove arm bends and tucks the glove near the left hip and she snaps the wrist to complete the throw. (See figure 5.4.)

Underhand Throw

This throw is usually made from the fielding position. The key to the forehand toss, which is part of the underhand throw, is to stay low to the ground with knees and waist bent. With the ball in the right hand, the athlete keeps the arm straight and in a pendulum motion,

FIGURE 5.4
The side-arm throw.

swinging the arm back to but not above waist level. At this point, the hand should be behind the ball. The fielder steps toward the target with her left foot and swings her right arm forward, pushing the ball toward the target. Be careful not to snap the wrist or bend the fingers. The ball should be tossed at the waist level of the receiver. (See figure 5.5.)

Backhand Toss

The backhand toss is also made from the fielding position. The fielder keeps low to the ground and fields the ball with two hands. While gripping the ball, she rotates her throwing hand around to a position inside the ball. She then steps toward the target with her right foot and leads the toss with a bent right elbow. Her wrist and forearm remain stiff as the ball is pushed toward the target with the fingers. She should be careful not to flip the wrist or bend her fingers. The ball is flipped at the waist level of the receiver. (See figure 5.6.)

FIGURE 5.5
The forehand toss.

FIGURE 5.6
The backhand toss.

HOW TO CATCH

Every player on the team must learn to catch effectively. Visual acuity and anticipatory skills are crucial to the athlete in determining the correct location and subsequent body position for making a catch.

Players should receive the ball on the midline of the body using two hands to make the catch whenever possible. This reduces the risk of mishandling or dropping the ball and also aids the defensive player in preparing to make the throw much more quickly. It is sometimes impossible to catch the ball on the midline and with two hands. In these instances, players should use a forehand catch (see figure 5.7) to reach for a ball on the glove side of the body, and a backhand catch (see figure 5.8) to reach for a ball on the throwing side of the body.

Glove Positioning

Glove positioning varies for balls in different locations. Any ball caught above the waist should be received with the fingers of both hands pointing up, with the hands positioned thumb-to-thumb (see figure 5.9). The fingers of both hands should point to the ground on balls caught below the waist, with the hands positioned little finger-to-little finger (see figure 5.10). As soon as the ball enters the glove, the throwing hand should secure the ball immediately for the catch.

Glove positioning is of particular importance with younger players. Beginners have a tendency to catch *all* balls with the palm of the glove facing up. This becomes dangerous on balls arriving at face level. The ball often travels right over the outstretched arm and into the face of the player. The glove must be in a position to stop the ball at this level. If this seems problematic, try the following: Ask your

THROWING DRILLS

Finding the Seam

Have two players play catch. Player A receives, or catches the ball with two hands. As she rotates her body to move to the throwing position, she takes the ball back past her throwing shoulder to set up the throwing hand for the throw. During this action, where she takes the ball back past her shoulder, she rotates her hand over the top of the ball, using her fingers to feel for the seam on the ball. She should practice this maneuver as she plays catch to get into the habit of finding the seam on the ball for the proper grip in preparation to throw. As a progression, initially allow your athletes to look at the ball as the hand rotates over it to find the seam. (It's okay if they stop to look at the ball at first. However, this should be one continuous motion from receiving the ball to taking it back to throw.) When your athletes have mastered that, tell them not to look at the ball as they take it back to throw. Have them find the seam by feel only.

Quick-Snap Throws

Instruct athletes to partner up and kneel on one knee (the throwing side knee) about 10 feet apart from one another. Player A starts with her glove hand pointing at Player B and her throwing arm in the quick-snap starting position. Player A uses her forearm, wrist, and fingers to snap the ball to her partner. Player B then repeats the drill.

players which hand signal they would use to get somebody to stop walking toward them. Using the glove hand without the glove on, have them show you the hand signal, saying "stop" several times. Then ask them to put their gloves on and show you the same hand signal (using the glove hand and saying, "stop!"). Emphasize the importance of using this signal with an incoming ball above the waist.

Body Positioning

Proper body positioning is essential for infielders making force outs at the bases on the infield. Although much emphasis is put on how the first baseman receives the throw at first base, this same technique should be used by all the infielders receiving throws at any of the

One-Knee Throws

Have athletes partner up and kneel on one knee (the throwing side knee) about 20 feet away from one another. Player A starts with both hands together at chest level. She separates her hands and executes the entire over-hand throwing motion with the upper body only. Player B then repeats drill. **Variation:** Change overhand throwing motion to side-arm throws.

Forehand Tosses

Position any number of infielders in a line about 30 feet away from the coach or other player who will be the target. The target rolls the ball to the first player in line, who charges the ball, then fields the ball, and, staying low, uses a forehand toss to throw to the target. Repeat the drill with the next player in line. Players move to the end of the line.

Backhand Tosses

Have athletes partner up and stand approximately 15 feet apart. One athlete starts with the ball and drops it on the ground in front between her feet. She must drop to her fielding position and execute the backhand toss to her partner. Her partner repeats the drill.

FIGURE 5.7
The forehand catch.

FIGURE 5.8
The backhand catch.

FIGURE 5.9
Glove positioning for a catch above
the waist.

FIGURE 5.10
Glove positioning for a catch below
the waist.

bases in a force-out situation. Proper execution of the first baseman's "stretch," as it is sometimes called, can make the difference between a safe or out call at the base.

Coaching Tip

Defensive players must move their feet to catch the ball on the body's midline. If players stand and catch with one hand repeatedly, they'll get lazy. When defense gets lazy, balls get dropped and performance suffers. This can hurt team morale, so let your expectations be known.

In preparing to receive the throw, the infielder should remain balanced and be positioned on the ball side of the bag. Her feet should be about hip-width apart and her heels should be within a few inches of the edge of the base. It is important to note that the infielder waits until the throw is made before going into any kind of a stretch to receive the ball. If the throw is significantly offline and wide of the bag, the infielder can leave the base to make the catch and stop the ball from becoming an overthrow. If the infielder commits to a stretch too early, she will not be able to move well enough to stop a bad throw. When the throw has been made, the infielder can then begin to position herself to make the catch.

The infielder should catch the ball as far out in front of her body as possible. She places the ball of her throwing side foot along the inside edge (not on top) of the base and steps toward the throw with her glove side foot. She then takes a large stride toward the ball but still remains balanced and able to make the catch. She then reaches out with both arms extended to make the catch with two hands.

HOW TO FIELD GROUND BALLS

Defensive players are required to field balls hit on the ground. They must be quick to read the ball off the bat and move to get the body in the best position to make the stop. When getting the ball on the midline of the body is not possible, forehand and backhand techniques must be used. Your athletes must learn to be as efficient as possible when fielding the ball in order to reduce the chance of runners reaching base.

Ready Position

A good ready position for fielding ground balls consists of keeping the body low to the ground with the feet apart so that a quick move can be made wherever the ball is hit. The feet should be wider than hip-width apart and both knees should be bent (see figure 5.11). The fielder should have the feeling of sitting slightly, and her hands should be close to the ground. Her head should be up and her eyes should be focused on the ball.

FIGURE 5.11
The ready position.

Getting to the Ball

Very seldom is the ball hit directly at a player so that she doesn't have to move. If the ball is hit slowly in front of her, she should charge the ball. If she must move in either direction laterally, she should use one or more side steps (shuffle), or use a crossover step to get to a ball hit hard on her backhand (throwing) side (see figure 5.12). She should receive a ball hit straight on with her feet

---

PLAYING AGAINST THE SUN

Teach your athletes how to field a fly ball hit into the sun. Players should be aware ahead of time of a sun hazard on a fly ball in their area. This condition may change as the game progresses, so players must be alert. When there is a sun hazard, the fielders should get into the habit of blocking the sun with their gloves on any ball hit overhead. This way, they are not caught off guard on a ball that gets lost in the sun when they weren't expecting it to. Teach the following technique for blocking the sun: When the ball goes up, immediately put the glove hand up in the air with the arm extended and the glove in its closed position. The back of the glove (fingers) should be nearest the sky. Use the glove to cover the sun to avoid being "blinded" by the sunlight. A shadow appears over the eye area on the player's face when done correctly. Move the edge of the glove to the edge of the sun to see as much of the sky as possible. When the player sees the ball, she should move under it, bring the glove around to its open position, and make the catch above the forehead, using both hands.

FIGURE 5.12
Crossover step to backhand side.

FIGURE 5.13
Fielding position.

slightly staggered, so that the left foot is ahead of the right foot. Her feet should be apart, and the ball should be fielded slightly out front, and on the midline of her body (see figure 5.13). Watching the ball all the way into the glove is crucial and her hands should be held little finger-to-little finger. As soon as the ball moves into the glove, she should secure it with her throwing hand.

Preparing to Throw

Without breaking her momentum, the fielder should bring the ball up across her body with two hands and back past the shoulder to throw (see figure 5.14). She should take as few steps as is necessary to get into position to throw. Follow the steps outlined for overhand throwing. This is where time is of the essence for fielders. The longer they hold the ball, the further the runner advances.

FIGURE 5.14
Preparing to throw.

Forehand Play

If a ball is hit hard on the ground to a player's glove side, she should use the forehand technique for fielding a ground ball. From the ready position, she should take a crossover step to her glove side and remain bent at the waist while quickly moving to intercept the ball. The infielder should reach out with her glove arm fully extended to field the ball and then position her body for the throw. (See figure 5.15.)

Backhand Play

When the ball is hit hard to the throwing side, the backhand technique should be used. From the ready position, the player takes a crossover step with the foot starting on the opposite side of the ball.

CATCHING DRILLS

Footballs

Bring a few *small* footballs to practice. Have your players partner up to play catch with the footballs. Players won't need gloves. This exercise teaches players to use two hands on the catch, and teaches the use of proper finger positions when catching balls above and below the waist. **Variations:** Use softee balls, table-tennis balls, or other small balls that are safe to use without a glove.

Quick Catch and Throw (for Older Players)

Have your players partner up and stand 30 feet away from one another to play catch. They should catch and throw to one another as quickly as possible to work on throwing and catching skills.

Line Drill

Have any number of players form a single line about 40 feet from the coach. The coach throws a ball to the first person in line at a position above the waist. The player must use the proper glove and hand position to make an above-the-waist catch. She throws the ball back to the coach and goes to the end of the line. The drill is repeated with the next player in line. **Variation:** Throw balls below the waist. Give one point for each correct catch. Make a game of it!

FIGURE 5.15
Crossover step to forehand side and forehand play.

The waist should remain bent and the fielder should move quickly to intercept the ball. She should extend her glove arm fully to field the ball just off the left foot. She should step one more time with her right foot and plant it firmly to stop her momentum from taking her further in that direction. She should then be able to step toward the target with her left foot to begin the throw. (See figure 5.16.)

Outfield Variation

Outfielders may use a different approach to the ball than infielders. Because of the greater distances involved in playing the outfield, outfielders should approach a ground ball head on whenever possible. When a ball is hit to either side of an outfielder, she should begin to move laterally and angle slightly back if necessary to "circle" the ball and field it while moving toward the infield (see figure 5.17).

HOW TO FIELD FLY BALLS

Fly balls can be more difficult to field because they are airborne. Ground balls generally require fielders to move only forward or

FIGURE 5.16
Backhand play.

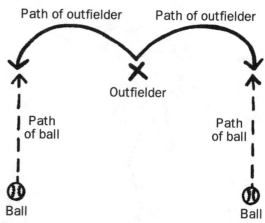

FIGURE 5.17
An outfielder's approach to a ground ball hit to either side.

sideways. Fly balls have the added element of going deep and requiring fielders to drop back to cover territory behind them. Fielders may have difficulty distinguishing between a fly ball that is hit high but short versus a ball hit high and deep over head. The first situation requires players to act quickly to move in to catch the ball while the latter requires

CROW-HOP

Teach your outfielders how to crow-hop. The crow-hop is an outfield technique used in the windup to help the athlete throw farther. The athlete moves forward (toward the intended target) into the ball when fielding it. Upon fielding the ball, her glove side foot is slightly forward of the other foot. She leaps up into the air slightly and onto her throwing side foot, followed by a quick step forward with the glove-side foot to throw forcefully. The crow-hop uses forward momentum to leap vertically to build up even more momentum coming down into the throw. This takes practice, but is highly beneficial to outfielders. Have your athletes practice without gloves and balls first. Place two bats on the ground parallel to one another, about one foot apart. Let them practice leaping from their glove side feet onto their throwing side feet followed by the quick step to throw.

them to act decisively to drop back to retrieve the ball.

Fielding Position

Whenever possible, the player should position herself directly under the ball to make the catch. The fly ball is received with two hands thumb-to-thumb, directly above the forehead. The left foot should be slightly staggered and ahead of the right foot on the catch. (See figure 5.18.)

FIGURE 5.18
Fielding a fly ball.

Dropping Back

A defensive player should use a drop step to move back on a ball hit over her head. From her ready position, she steps with the foot that is on the side the ball is hit. For example, if the fly ball is hit up over her right shoulder, then she executes the drop step with her right foot (see figure 5.19).

Assume the ball is hit over the athlete's right shoulder. The step begins with shifting the body weight to the left foot. The right foot is raised, and the entire body turns to open to the right. The right foot is placed down on the ground with the toe pointing straight back behind the fielder, exactly opposite its starting position. The athlete pushes off of her left foot and begins to run back on the ball.

If possible, the athlete should keep visual contact with the ball. If that is not possible, she should periodically head check, or take quick looks up to track the ball. If a ball is hit so hard overhead that she knows she can't make the catch, she should drop step back, put her head down and run as hard as she can to return to the probable vicinity of its landing spot. Periodic head checks are necessary to remain on course with the ball's trajectory.

FIGURE 5.19
The drop step.

Playing the Angle

Playing the angle on a ball is extremely important to get to the ball as fast as possible. For a ball hit hard to either side of the player, a deep angle is necessary to cut the ball off before it gets by the fielder. If the angle is too shallow, the ball will get by the athlete, and she'll have a longer distance to run to recover it. (See figure 5.20.)

HOW TO PITCH

Pitching in fast-pitch softball is a highly specialized skill requiring much practice for mastery. For that reason, younger players may have rule modifications that will allow for pitching variations in youth play. The youngest players (ages 7 to 8) usually start out playing tee ball, which requires no pitching at all. As players get older, you may use a pitching machine, or games may be played whereby coaches do the pitching. Your league or organization has information on pitching modifications for your level of play. A serious pitcher, however, usually finds a pitching instructor for private lessons sometime during her career. It takes a high level of dedication and commitment to effectively master the art of pitching.

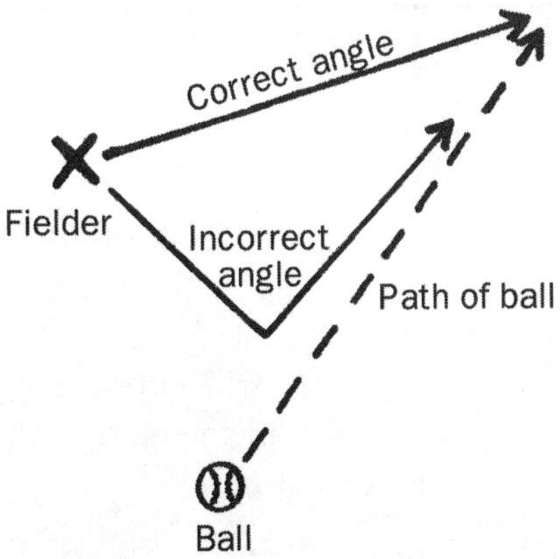

FIGURE 5.20
The correct and incorrect angles to the ball.

It is the pitcher's job to throw a softball using an underhand motion to a batter standing at home plate. The more velocity and movement on the ball, the harder it is for the batter to hit. There is an area called the strike zone that consists of the vertical space above home plate between the batter's armpits and the top of her knees (see your rulebook for strike zone specifications for your level of play). When the pitcher pitches the ball into this zone, a strike is called on the batter if the batter doesn't hit the ball. If the pitcher misses the strike zone with a pitch, a ball is called on the batter, as long as the batter doesn't swing. After three strikes, the batter is out, or after four balls, the batter draws a walk and gets a free trip to first base.

Historically, the figure eight, slingshot, and windmill styles of delivery have been used to pitch in women's fast-pitch softball. Although you may see an occasional slingshot delivery used today, the windmill style has become the preferred style of pitching. The key to the windmill style is to make the arm circle big and keep the circle in the same plane as the line to home plate. If the edge of the windmill plane deviates from a straight line to home plate, accuracy will be affected. The windmill delivery is generally accepted as the best way to get maximum velocity and movement on the ball when it is pitched underhand.

DRILLS

Grounders

Have athletes form one line, standing about 30 feet away from the coach. The coach rolls the ball on the ground to the first person in line, who must charge the ball and field it on the midline of the body. Once the ball is secured, she throws it back to the coach and goes to the end of the line. Repeat the drill with the next player in line. **Variations:** (1) Do the same thing with partners. (2) Add movement by rolling the ball to the forehand side for forehand plays and to the backhand side for backhand plays.

Side to Side

Have athletes partner up and stand about 10 feet from one another. Designate one person the fielder and the other the tosser. The fielder takes a good ready position. The tosser rolls a ball on the ground to one side of the fielder. The fielder must move laterally, using side steps (shuffle) to field the ball on the midline of the body and toss it underhand back to the tosser. The tosser immediately rolls the ball (easily) on the ground back in the other direction. The fielder shuffles to get the ball on the midline and tosses it underhand to the tosser. Switch positions between partners. Control the drill so the fielder has to move but is able to get to the ball on the midline. This is also a good conditioning drill.

Ball rotation or spin dictates movement on the ball. When there is no movement on the ball but only top end velocity, the pitch is known as a fastball. All other pitches are variations of a fastball and depend upon the ball's speed and spin. The seams on the ball play an important role in spin. When the pitcher uses a certain grip so that four seams are rotating, or "biting," into the air, ball movement can be significant. Specific pitches and how to throw them will be addressed at the end of this section. The basic pitching mechanics, however, will be for the windmill style of delivery when throwing a fastball. Once again, we will assume a right-handed thrower.

The Grip

The ball is gripped in the fingers and thumb of the right hand and not pushed into the palm. The three middle fingers are spread out so that the pads of the fingertips are on the seam, which allows a four-seam rotation upon release (see figure 5.21). The four-seam rotation can be established by doing the following: Turn the ball and follow the seam until it forms a large letter "C" (see inset of figure 5.21). Place the fingers along the top of the "C." As the ball is released off of the fingers, all four seams will rotate around the ball. The same grip can be established with the letter "C" reading backward. The little finger fits comfortably alongside the ball to help with stability and trajectory. The thumb is placed on the ball opposite the fingers. Younger players may have to use four fingers on the ball due to their smaller hands. The thumb should be placed in a comfortable position to grip the ball. The thumb is the "steering wheel" for the pitch. Therefore, you should lead the thumb in the direction you want the ball to go. For example, if you want to throw the ball on the inside of the plate, aim the thumb at the inside edge of home plate.

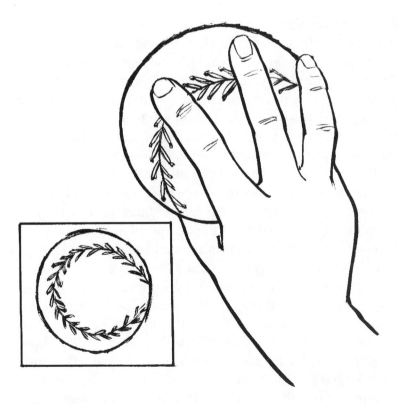

FIGURE 5.21
The fastball grip used in pitching.

The Stance

The pitcher begins by comfortably standing with both feet in contact with the pitcher's plate about hip-width apart. The ball of the right foot, which will be the pivot foot, rests along the front edge of the plate. The ball of the left foot, or stride foot, is in contact with the back edge of the plate. Both feet must be within the side edges of the pitcher's plate as well. The body weight is predominantly on the front foot. The hands are apart with the ball positioned in either hand, arms comfortably at the sides of the body (see figure 5.22). It is at this point that the pitcher sees the signal from the catcher, which indicates what type of pitch is being called.

The Pitch

FIGURE 5.22
Taking the signal.

After taking the signal from the catcher, the pitcher then shifts her weight to the back foot and brings her hands together in front of the body. This position must be held for at least one second. The pitcher begins by shifting her weight forward onto her right foot. As she strides toward home plate with her left foot, both hands move together to a position with arms extended horizontal to the ground in front of the body. The glove arm remains horizontal, and the throwing arm moves to a vertical position with the ball directly overhead. The hand should be on the inside of the ball facing third base. The right foot pivots to allow the shoulders and hips to open to the right side so that the belt buckle faces third base. This position is commonly referred to as the "K" position, because when viewed from third base, the body looks almost like the letter "K."

With the hips open, the pitcher continues the windmill motion with the throwing hand, arm extended, by bringing it around past the right hip with the ball at the mid-thigh area. As the arm passes the right hip, the glove hand and arm pull back and curl along the left side of the body. After pushing off the mound, the right elbow bends, allowing the wrist to snap through the ball. The ball should roll off of the fingertips. The follow-through will act to dissipate the forces generated by the pitch to help reduce the risk of injury to the throwing arm and body. (See figure 5.23.)

FIGURE 5.23
The windmill pitch.

The Follow-Through

After releasing the ball, the right hip closes in behind the ball, finishing so that the belt buckle faces home plate. The right hand finishes over the shoulder near the ear with the elbow bent. The pitcher steps through with her right leg to bring her body into a fielding position. Since the pitcher is often the defensive player closest to the batter, she should be ready to field the ball as quickly as possible.

How to Throw Different Pitches

Younger players, ages 7 to 10, should focus on basic pitching mechanics and throw fastballs. It is at these earlier ages that players learn to acquire speed and accuracy. When pitchers reach the age of 11, provided they have command of the basics, they may begin to experiment with throwing various pitches. The pitches discussed here are the drop, rise, and change-up. A pitcher can be very successful having command of only two pitches as long as she can throw to locations in the strike zone extremely well.

The Drop Ball

The drop ball is the easiest pitch to learn for a developing pitcher. The pitch travels toward home plate and then tails down and can be difficult to hit. It can be an effective pitch because batters tend to hit the ball on the ground. As long as the defense can field ground balls, it keeps the risk of the long ball down and becomes a ground game on the infield.

The correct spin on the ball should be from bottom to top (from the pitcher's point of view). The grip consists of the three middle fingers comfortably spread apart on a seam to get the four-seam rotation (mentioned earlier in the pitching section addressing the grip). The thumb is on a seam on the side opposite the fingers. When the ball is released, the thumb is on top of the ball and the fingers are underneath it (see figure 5.24).

The pitcher takes a shorter stride toward home plate with the stride leg and snaps the fingers up behind the ball to get maximum spin. The ball should roll off the fingertips.

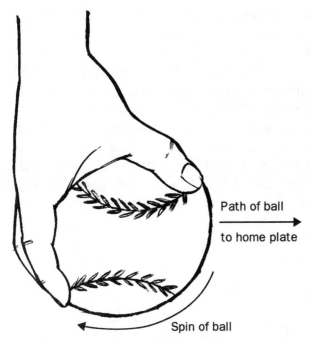

Path of ball
to home plate

Spin of ball

FIGURE 5.24
The drop ball grip upon release.

The Rise Ball

The rise ball travels toward home plate and then appears to jump over the bat. If this pitch doesn't break well, it may be thrown into the strike zone. Balls that enter the strike zone high are likely to travel out high, which can mean giving up extra base hits and home runs. If a pitcher doesn't have good command of the rise ball, it can be thrown as a "show" pitch, which means that the pitcher wants to throw it just to keep the hitter aware that she'll throw into that part of the strike zone. When the pitch is thrown to "show" it, it is important to make sure the ball is thrown up out of the strike zone.

The correct spin for the rise ball is to get the four seams rotating from top to bottom (from the pitcher's point of view). It is similar to putting a backspin on the ball. The grip consists of laying the index finger on its side along a seam. The other three fingers are spaced comfortably around the ball, with the thumb along an adjacent seam opposite the index finger (see figure 5.25). When the pitch is released, the wrist should be flexed and the index finger should apply pressure to the seam. Upon release, the action is similar to turning a doorknob as if to open a door.

To throw the rise ball, the player takes a slightly longer stride toward home plate with the stride leg. Upon release, she allows the wrist to rotate inward so that the thumb is on top and the fingers are under the ball. The palm faces to the side, away from the body. The fingers snap hard under the ball (look for the four-seam rotation), applying pressure to the seams with the thumb and index finger. Upon follow-through, the elbow should bend sharply with the hand finishing at a point just above the right shoulder.

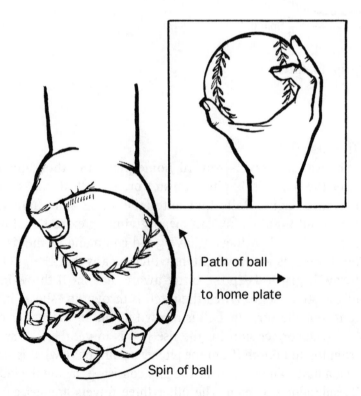

Path of ball
to home plate

Spin of ball

FIGURE 5.25
The rise ball grip.

The Change-Up

The change-up is very effective because it travels toward home plate at a much slower speed than the other pitches and, thus, fools the batter. Hitting is timing, and a hitter is conditioned to swing based upon the pitcher's motion. From a batter's point of view, the change-up looks like a high velocity pitch destined for the strike zone. The hitter is fooled, however, and begins her swing too early to hit the ball.

The grip for the change-up is simple, but like all of the other pitches, it takes practice to throw it well. The ball is held in the palm of the hand using all four fingers and the thumb to secure it in place (see figure 5.26). The speed of the pitcher's arm circle is the same as for any other pitch (this is key for fooling the batter). Upon release, the wrist stiffens and the fingers straighten so that the ball pops out of the hand. After releasing the ball, the hand should continue forward and follow-through at the same speed as with throwing any other pitch.

HOW TO CATCH A PITCH

Catching in fast-pitch softball is a huge responsibility. In addition to fielding the position itself, the catcher must decide what pitches to call and what locations in the strike zone are most effective in working against each batter. The catcher must tune into the pitcher's demeanor, keep her steady on the mound, and know what pitches are working and which ones aren't. She has to have a good head on her

FIGURE 5.26
The change-up grip.

shoulders and be willing to endure the strenuousness of the position, be it blocking out balls in the dirt or bracing for a collision at home plate from an incoming runner.

There is an art to catching. It is a position that handles the ball on nearly every pitch, and it involves a lot of up and down legwork. A catcher can't afford to be lazy. She must alter her position when runners are on base and throw them out when they attempt to steal. The catcher has a great deal of responsibility. After all, it is partly her job to keep runners from reaching home plate.

Ready Position

In the ready position, the catcher takes a position as close to home plate as possible without interfering with the swing of the batter. The closer she is to home plate, the greater the chance there is of the ball being called a strike, and the sooner she receives the ball, the sooner she can make a play on a runner attempting to steal.

Down Position

The catcher may assume a "down" position only when there aren't any runners on base. In the down position, the catcher is in a squat

PITCHING DRILLS

"K" Position Pitching

Have the pitcher stand approximately 15 feet away from a fence and provide her with a bucket of balls. Give her a ball and start her in the "K" position. Have her finish the arm circle to complete the pitch using correct body mechanics and end up in a fielding position. **Variation:** Tape a target on the fence and have her hit the target area. Award points for hitting the target area. Make a game of it!

Snap Drill

Have the pitcher hold the ball in the pitching hand using the correct grip for the pitch to be practiced. Standing, have her start her forearm parallel to the ground, holding the ball in front of the body. She flicks the ball up into the air in front of her, practicing the wrist snap up and through the ball. She should be able to control the ball so that it comes back down to her.

with the feet approximately hip-width apart (see figure 5.27). The weight is on the balls of her feet, and the glove hand is extended away from the body to give the pitcher a large target. The throwing hand is protected by positioning the hand and arm comfortably behind the back or behind the throwing side leg.

Up Position

The catcher should assume an "up" position when there are runners on base. Her feet are approximately hip-width apart with the feet staggered slightly for the throw (left foot ahead of the right foot for a right-handed thrower). The catcher's back is nearly parallel to the ground with the back portion of her body raised. Her throwing hand is protected by positioning the hand and arm comfortably behind the back or behind the throwing side leg (see figure 5.28). This allows a quick transfer of the ball to the throwing hand should the need arise to throw quickly.

Throwing Out Runners

When a runner steals a base, the catcher receives the ball from the pitcher while stepping and transferring her body weight to her back

Speed Drill

Have the pitcher stand about 30 feet away from a catcher. Give the pitcher a ball and have her walk into a pitch and pitch the ball as fast as she can to the catcher. The catcher throws the ball back as fast as she can overhand. As soon as the pitcher receives the ball, she pitches it again as fast as she can. Repeat this 15 times. This also works well for conditioning.

Arm Circles

Have the pitcher stand in her stride position, so that the belt buckle faces third base (for a right-handed thrower). Practice the arm circle, concentrating on full extension, by whipping the arm around, making arm circles in rapid succession. **Variation:** Stand in front of a fence and add a ball to the pitching hand. Make five rapid arm circles and release the ball on a pitch straight into the fence.

FIGURE 5.27
The down position for catchers.

FIGURE 5.28
The up position for catchers.

foot. She takes the glove hand back to meet her throwing hand over the opposite shoulder to a point just behind the ear. She then steps toward the base to make the throw.

Giving Signals

Signals, or combinations of numbers, tell the pitcher to throw specific pitches. These numbers may correspond to specific pitches and locations in the strike zone. Signals are given to the pitcher from the down position. With a runner on base, the signal is given in the down position first, and then the catcher positions herself in the up position. The signals are given with the knees apart and the fingers of the throwing hand spread as far apart as possible up against the crotch of the pants so the pitcher can see the signs. The glove is positioned on the outside of the glove side leg just above the ankle to block the signals from being seen by the third base coach.

Blocking Balls

From time to time, pitches are thrown into the dirt before they reach the catcher's glove. If the catcher can effectively block the ball and keep it in front of her body, the baserunners are likely to hesitate and won't be able to advance to the next base. When the catcher realizes the ball is going to hit the dirt, she stays low and positions her body in front of the ball to get the ball on the midline of her body. She drops to her knees and puts her glove hand down between her knees to block the space between her legs (see figure 5.29). She tucks her chin to her chest and keeps her eyes on the ball. If the pitch is to her glove side, she steps out to the side with that foot to keep the ball in the center of her body and drags the trailing leg along side while using her glove to block the space between her legs. She should use the same technique to balls pitched in the dirt to the other side.

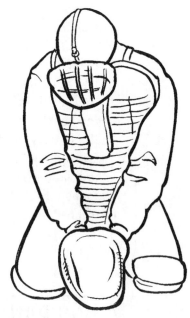

FIGURE 5.29
Catcher blocking a ball correctly.

Receiving Throws for a Tag Play

After the ball is hit, the catcher takes a position in front of home plate with her left foot at the third base edge of the plate. Her body faces the direction of the throw, and she receives the throw with both hands. After receiving the throw, she turns toward the runner and stays low to the ground in preparation to make the tag. After making the tag, she should be attentive to trail runners, unless that is the third out of the inning.

Receiving Throws for a Force Play

After the ball is hit, the catcher moves to a position in front of home plate with her body facing the throw. She places her throwing side foot on the front of the plate and steps toward the ball with the glove side leg and glove hand to receive the throw with two hands. After the catch, she prepares to make a play on any trail runners, unless it was the third out of the inning.

You should plan to spend a great deal of time developing your players' individual skills. Although softball is a team sport, each athlete must have proficient throwing, catching, and fielding skills. It is impossible to play defense without them. Pitchers and catchers are the backbone of the team and handle the ball on every play. They are the battery, and because they handle the ball so often, they need to know how to effectively handle themselves in games. When each individual has command of the basics, team defense can be addressed focusing on how players work together to thwart the efforts of the offense.

CATCHING DRILLS

Face Mask Drill

To get your catcher used to keeping her eyes open with the mask on, have her wear the mask and stand about two feet away from the coach or tosser. Start with tennis balls and toss them into her mask, watching her eyes to make sure she keeps them open. Graduate to softballs.

Blocking Drill for Body Angle

Put the catcher in full gear and have her start in the down position about 4 to 5 feet away from the tosser or coach. Have her put both arms behind her back and clasp her wrist with her other hand. Toss the ball low into her body protector and have her drop to her blocking position. Challenge her by backing up a little farther and toss balls a little farther out to the side of her, still chest high. She must learn to get her body out in front of the ball and turn her torso to get the ball to rebound back toward home plate.

Receiving Throws at Home

As the coach, take a bat and a bucket of balls to a position in the baseline somewhere on the infield. Hit balls at the catcher one at a time to simulate throws from fielders. Ground balls with two or three hops are realistic throws from outfielders and should be practiced. In each case, the catcher must receive the ball and make a tag.

6

THE HOW-TO'S OF INDIVIDUAL OFFENSIVE PLAY

EVERY YOUNG BALL player dreams of walking up to home plate with the game on the line, and then hitting a dramatic home run to win the ball game. Delivering the game winning hit and being mobbed by teammates is one of those great moments in sports that we've all witnessed at one time or another. When a team gets hot on offense, there's usually a great deal of excitement!

Defense will keep a team in a ball game, but it takes offense to win. There have been times when my teams have played tough on defense only to lose in the end because we couldn't push a run across the plate. Games like that are frustrating, and I usually devote the next practice to hitting. I set up hitting stations, hitting machines, live batting practice, and everything we can muster to beef up run production for the next game. A practice like that certainly makes us feel better, and ultimately, I believe that it helps us become better hitters.

Like defense, the offensive part of the game relies upon the skills of individual players working together to score runs. Occasionally there is the home run, where one player hits the ball, touches all the bases, and scores a run all by herself, but generally, it takes several players combining all of their offensive efforts to push a run or two across the plate. Batting involves a great deal of technique. If certain laws of physics are violated when batting, it won't matter how much batting practice a player gets, she'll never be a good hitter. For example, the arms and bat work as levers during the batting swing. When the batter hits the ball, she gets the most out of her swing when her arms are fully extended as the barrel of the bat collides with the ball. For maximum force to be generated to change the direction of the ball, the batter should have a straight line from the tip of her front shoulder down through the end of the bat. If her arms or wrists are bent as the bat collides with the ball, she will lose power in her swing and not be able to generate the maximum force to hit the ball effectively, no matter how much batting practice she takes. Every player on the team also needs to know how to bunt, as it is a huge part of the offensive game in fast-pitch softball. If your players can't bunt, you'll have a hard time advancing baserunners. Finally, your players need to understand the intricacies of baserunning and how to slide correctly. Spending time with individual players to develop their proficiency in executing these offensive skills is essential.

HOW TO BAT

The goal of batting in softball is to hit a round object with another round object, squarely. In trying to understand how difficult that feat may be, take a look at a batting average. A hitter with a .300 batting average is considered a good hitter in fast-pitch softball. But when you realize that this .300 hitter has failed in 7 of 10 attempts to hit safely, it gives you a better appreciation for the skill.

When teaching young girls how to hit, it is important to emphasize good basics in the stance, swing, and follow-through. Through many repetitions in practice, young players will likely develop their own styles of hitting, and should be allowed to do so, as long as style doesn't interfere with the proper mechanics of the swing.

The Stance

The batter should position herself in the middle of the batter's box and square to home plate. The batter's belt buckle should be lined up with the center of the plate, and adjustments may be made from there. A player will want to move up in the box (closer to the pitcher) if the pitching is too slow, and back in the box (closer to the catcher) if it is too fast. Hitting is timing, and good hitters make adjustments with each pitch. These adjustments, based upon the speed of pitching, help the hitter with her timing.

The bat should be held comfortably in the fingers, and not squeezed tight in the palms of the hands. Ideally, the middle knuckles (door-knocking knuckles) of both hands should be lined up to give the hitter a good wrist roll though the swing. If the hitter is comfortable with the bat but needs to swing it a little quicker because she is facing faster pitching, she should "choke up," or move her hands a little farther away from the knob. Otherwise, her hand position should be at or near the knob of the bat.

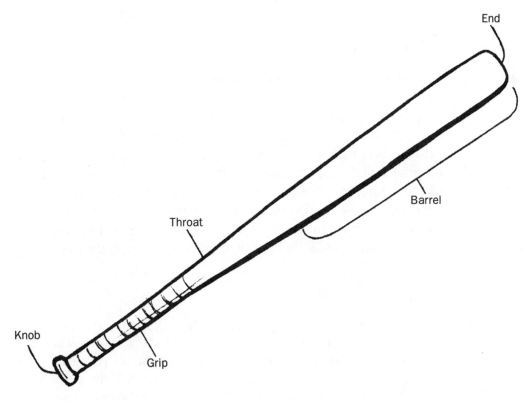

FIGURE 6.1
Anatomy of a softball bat.

Good support in the stance will aid the batter in maintaining balance throughout the swing. The feet should be approximately hip-width apart with the body weight evenly distributed along the inside and on the balls of the feet (avoid putting too much weight on the heels). The knees should be slightly bent and the hitter should bend gently forward at the waist, giving the player a sense of slightly sitting to hit the ball. With both hands gripping the bat, the arms should be in such a position as to allow the barrel of the bat to sit just above the back shoulder (approximately 6 inches). The bat should be held approximately 45 degrees back over the shoulder, yet comfortably upright. The front arm should be slightly bent and the elbow of the back arm should be up and to the rear, yet in a comfortable position. (See figure 6.2.) Visually focusing the eyes on the pitcher's mid-thigh area should cause the head to rotate forward to a comfortable position as well.

The Swing

The softball swing is a short, compact stroke down through the ball. Because the pitch is delivered from the mid-thigh area with an underhand motion, it tends to travel toward the plate with an upward trajectory. (See figure 6.3.) Consequently, a slight downswing through the ball will best match the trajectory of a pitch thrown slightly upward toward the plate and will give the hitter the greatest impact zone possible. It also means a better chance of hitting the ball. In baseball, the pitch is delivered with an overhand motion, and the trajectory is slightly downward toward the plate. A batter in baseball has the greatest impact zone possible with a slight upswing through the ball.

PLAYER'S STANCE

When working with young girls on any base of support having to do with how far apart the feet should be, using the phrase "hip-width apart" isn't that critical. With younger girls, the hips and shoulders are generally about the same in body width. As girls reach menarche and their bodies begin to change, reference to the feet being "hip-width apart," instead of "shoulder-width apart," will take on more significance and have clearer meaning. When a young female's body changes, so does her center of gravity and as a result, standing with the feet "hip-width apart" will provide her with a better base of support.

FIGURE 6.2
Batting stance.

FIGURE 6.3
A slight downswing through the ball in fast-pitch softball will give the hitter the greatest impact zone when batting.

The proper sequence of batting begins with the feet and works its way up the body. The swing, when executed properly, is a power train of rotating joints, and each joint of the body (e.g., hips, shoulders, wrists, etc.) must operate in the correct order to provide the force necessary to hit a softball effectively. Certain laws of physics apply when hitting a softball, and if any part of the swing breaks down, the transfer of force and velocity that would otherwise be transferred from the bat to the ball is lost.

Hitting the ball begins with a small step or stride with the front foot. Each hitter, through many repetitions in practice, determines the timing of this step. Depending upon the speed of the pitch, this step is generally taken when the pitcher releases the ball. The stride should be directed toward the pitcher, and the foot should land at a 45-degree angle, splitting the 90-degree angle created by the front edge of home plate and a line drawn directly to the pitcher. For a right-handed batter, the toe points to where the second baseman stands at her position, and for a left-handed batter, the toe points to where the shortstop stands at her position.

When the stride is taken, several other functions occur simultaneously. As the batter picks up her foot to stride, body weight shifts slightly to the rear foot. The hips and hands rotate slightly in a posterior direction. As the front foot touches the ground, the body weight is focused along the inside edge of the foot. This point in the swing is often referred to as the launch position. In effect, there is a shift of weight and rotation of hands, shoulders, and hips slightly back to prepare the body to move forward. It is essentially a cocking action of various components of the body, components that must go backward in order to move forward.

Once the stride is taken, the hips begin to rotate. Good hip rotation is the key to a batter who hits for power. The rear leg aids in weight transfer and hip rotation. It is important to drive off the back leg and then pivot on the ball of the back foot. (Use the phrase "squish the bug" with the younger players to describe the pivoting action on the back foot.) As the hitter makes contact with the ball, the front leg straightens (but does not lock out at the knee). After the hitter drives through the ball, the front leg may bend and roll slightly. The back leg should form a backward "L" and stay in contact with the ground as the swing is completed. The hitter should still be balanced when finished and should be able to hold her position for a brief moment.

After the hips begin to rotate, the shoulders follow. The hands are held back and are the last component of the swing to fire forward. In the batting stance or starting position, the chin is positioned just inside the front shoulder. As the shoulders rotate around the body, the chin end ups positioned just inside the back shoulder that has now moved forward. If the chin goes shoulder to shoulder, this is a good indication that the head stayed down and the eyes remained on the ball throughout the swing.

As the shoulders rotate, the hands start toward the ball. The batter leads with the front elbow and takes the knob of the bat to the ball. This action with the knob of the bat enables the wrists to stay in a cocked position until they snap the bat head into the pitch. The player keeps her wrists cocked while making sure her hands stay inside the path of the ball and the bat head stays slightly higher than the pitch itself.

With this power train of rotating joints at optimum speed, the batter is now ready to drive the bat head into the ball for a base hit. The player extends both arms and snaps the wrists so that the bat head pops into the ball. On contact, the top hand is behind the bat (not rolled on top or under), and the front arm is nearly straight. The hitter should be able to draw an imaginary straight line from the tip of the front shoulder down through the arm and bat to the bat head. This is the optimum bat position for all of the force and speed generated by the body to be transferred from the bat to the ball. (See figure 6.4.)

Coaching Tip

A batter loses visual sight of the ball several feet in front of the plate. The athlete's ability to track the ball and anticipate where it will be in the strike zone allows a batter to make contact with the ball.

FIGURE 6.4
The batting swing.

The Follow-Through

A good follow-through is necessary for the body to safely dissipate all the forces generated by the body for the swing. After hitting the ball, the bat continues around the body and wraps around the back. The top hand remains on the bat and does not let go during the follow-through. If the hitter kept her eyes on the ball and her head down, her chin should have traveled shoulder to shoulder, and she should be balanced enough to hold the follow-through momentarily.

HOW TO BUNT

The bunt is a technique in fast-pitch softball that is used to get the ball down on the ground, usually in an area in front of home plate. There are five different kinds of bunts, and each is designed to accomplish a different objective. The sacrifice, push, squeeze, slap, and drag bunts are highly specialized in their execution and require extensive practice to perform effectively. Every player on your team should know how to execute the sacrifice, slap, and squeeze bunts. They vary only slightly in their execution yet can play a major role in the outcome of any game. The push bunt is merely an extension of the sacrifice bunt and has become sort of a lost art. This is likely due to the big play potential of the slap bunt when executed proficiently. Left-handed batters mostly use the drag bunt, but either way, it can be an effective tool for introducing an element of surprise into the game.

Sacrifice Bunt

A sacrifice bunt is used by the offense to give up an out to advance a baserunner. As its name implies, the batter/bunter bunts the ball down on the ground in front of home plate, in essence "sacrificing" herself, hoping the defense will make the play at first base to get her out instead of the baserunner. When that happens, the baserunner advances to the next base and is in a better scoring position if the next batter gets a base hit or if the defense makes an error and throws the ball away.

As with all bunts, the sacrifice bunt begins with the hitter's normal batting stance. From there, the bunt is broken down into the pivot, contact, and follow-through. When sacrifice bunting, it is important to bunt good pitches, that is, strikes. If the batter draws a walk instead, there's a bonus on the play. Not only does the baserunner end up advancing, but the batter also becomes a baserunner without giving up an out.

The Pivot

The batter takes a position "up" in the box, or closer to the pitcher, in her normal batting stance. Timing is important in determining when to pivot. After taking the signal from the catcher, the pitcher must "present the ball," meaning the hands must come together for a minimum of one second. When the pitcher's hands separate after presenting the ball, the batter should begin to pivot to bunt.

The batter pivots on both feet, turning so that her upper body is squared up to the pitcher (see figure 6.5). She bends at her knees and waist to bring her eyes more in line with the ball. As she pivots, she slides her top hand up the bat to the base of the barrel. Her bottom hand remains gripped on the bat as it was to hit, but the top hand forms a fist with the thumb cradling the bat opposite the index finger (see figure 6.6). This hand position allows for optimum bat control, yet protects the fingers from getting hit by the incoming pitch.

The bat is positioned parallel to the ground in front of the batter at the top of the strike zone. The arms are bent at the elbows and act as shock absorbers when the ball

FIGURE 6.5
The pivot to sacrifice bunt.

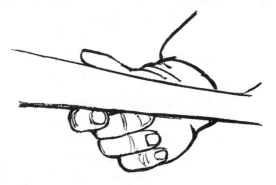

FIGURE 6.6
Top hand grip for the sacrifice bunt.

contacts the bat. The bat is at the top of strike zone to help the batter get the ball down. If the pitch comes in higher than the bat, the pitch will be a ball, and the batter needs only to pull the bat away. If the pitch comes in lower than the bat but in the strike zone, the batter then bends her knees to lower her body to bunt the ball.

Contact

The bunt is similar to "catching" the ball with the bat. The arms should give upon impact so that the ball doesn't rebound hard and turn into a ground ball easily fielded by the defense. The intent is to make the defense travel the distance to home plate and get to the ball

HITTING DRILLS

Soft Toss

The batter and tosser stand in front of a fence or screen. The batter assumes her normal batting stance, and the tosser drops to one knee at a spot about 4 to 5 feet away from the batter on the other side of home plate. The tosser gently throws a ball into the air, slightly in front of home plate. The batter hits the ball into the screen. Repeat. The tosser should be far enough away from the batter so the swinging bat won't hit her.

Hip Rotation and Pivot

The batter takes her stance and slips a bat behind her low back area, parallel to the ground, secured in place by her arms. Have her step to hit with her front foot while rotating her hips and pivoting on her back foot. The barrel of the bat should pass over the home plate area as the hips rotate through the swing. This drill will help the athlete work on the lower body portion of her swing. **Variation:** Add a soft toss, and have the batter stand in front of a fence or screen. She should hit the ball with the barrel of the bat and "pop" the ball (with hip action) into the screen.

Short, Compact Stroke

Have a batter take a bat and stand beside a fence or other flat surface. Have her place the end of the bat against the fence (the bat should be perpendicular to the fence) and stand close enough so that her tummy touches the end of the knob. She should maintain this distance from the fence and remain facing so that there is no time to make a play on the advancing baserunner—only the batter. It is important to teach the young player the significance of bending the knees while keeping the bat at eye level to get a low pitch that is a strike. The more the eyes stay lined up with the path of the incoming pitch and the bat, the greater the success of making contact with the ball and getting it down on the ground. (See figure 6.7.)

It is important to note that the ball may be bunted down either baseline rather easily. This is accomplished by pushing the bottom hand away from the body or pulling the bottom hand toward the body while it is on the bat grip. The top hand's grip on the bat will

the fence while taking a normal swing with the bat. If she hits the fence with the bat, she is probably casting her bat and she should shorten her swing. She must master a short, compact swing where she can take her normal step and swing without contacting the fence.

Balance

Lay a 2 × 6-inch piece of wood on the ground with the 6-inch side facing the ground. Have the batter stand on the wood and practice her complete swing. She should be able to remain balanced and stay on the 2 × 6 after completing her swing.

Tracking

Take an old softball and write the number "1" on it in several places so the number is about 3 inches in height. Take other balls and write different numbers on them in the same fashion (e.g., 4, 7, 8). Put the balls in a bucket. Stand about 8 to 10 feet in front of the batter and have her take her stance to hit. She should begin by looking at the ground. She should not look for the ball until you say "Now!" Take a ball out of the bucket and get ready to toss the ball into her strike zone. As you begin to toss the ball to her over the plate, say "Now!" and have her visually track the ball all the way in and try to read the number on the ball as it travels into her strike zone. SHE MUST NOT SWING THE BAT! When she can read the number, she should call it out. Repeat with the next ball. **Variation:** Use tennis balls.

FIGURE 6.7
Contact on the sacrifice bunt.

allow the bat to pivot, thereby providing the appropriate bat angle for placing the ball down either baseline. (See figure 6.8.)

The Follow-Through

Once the ball has been contacted, the batter should take great care not to interfere with the ball. Interference can occur if the batter runs into the ball en route to first base or drops the bat on the ball while discarding the bat to run. The player should discard the bat away from the ball and any defensive players moving in to make the play. She should run to first base only when the ball is safely out of the running lane.

Push Bunt

The push bunt is used to bunt the ball on the ground hard enough to get it past the incoming defensive fielder. The push bunt is highly

FIGURE 6.8
Top views of sacrifice bunt down first baseline (left) and down third baseline (right).

effective when the defense is aggressively defending the bunt by playing in close to home plate and charging hard to get to the ball quickly. It is executed exactly like the sacrifice bunt, except that on contact, the ball is pushed forcefully down onto the ground and past the charging corner player. The batter steps with the front foot in the direction of the push bunt while forcefully pushing the bat out away from her body and down into the ball in the direction she wants it to go (see figure 6.9).

FIGURE 6.9

Top view of push bunt, showing forceful pushing action of the bat at the ball.

Squeeze Bunt

The squeeze bunt is used to surprise the defense and score a runner from third base. It is very effective when the corners (first and third basemen) are playing back and are expecting the batter to swing away. It is a great weapon to use with your number three or four batter, because these slots in the batting order are typically used for top hitters. The corners on defense may back away from home plate to respect the batter's ability to hit the ball, and so the element of surprise can be highly effective.

The squeeze bunt is executed like the sacrifice bunt, except for two distinct differences. First, the batter squares at the moment the

PIVOT FOR THE BUNT

The timing of the pivot on the sacrifice, slap, and push bunts are the same—and it is always crucial. The key to the effectiveness of these three bunts is the element of surprise, in that the batter doesn't tip off the defense and give away the kind of bunt she's using. All of the bunts look the same initially, so the defense reacts to what it thinks is happening. When the sacrifice bunt is converted into the push bunt or the slap bunt, the defense is completely caught off guard and the element of surprise works in favor of the batter in executing the play.

ball leaves the pitcher's hand. As with all bunts, timing is the key to surprising the defense. Second, the batter must bunt the pitch, no matter where it is thrown. All other bunts are executed to bunt a strike only. The squeeze bunt, however, is executed with the next pitch, whatever the location. That is because the runner from third base is running home on the pitch. So it is essential that the batter makes every attempt to get the ball down on the ground.

Slap Bunt

The slap bunt is used to draw the defense in as if the batter were going to sacrifice bunt. But at the last minute, the batter pulls the bat back and hits the ball on the ground into either infield alley. The intent of the offense is that one of the middle infielders will vacate her position a little early, believing the batter is sacrifice bunting, and open up a hole on the infield for the ball to go through. As with the sacrifice bunt and the push bunt, the batter is looking for a good pitch (strike) to hit.

The timing and the pivot of the slap bunt are exactly the same as is used in executing the sacrifice bunt. The batter squares to face the pitcher when the pitcher's hands break apart and the batter should try to "sell" the sacrifice (make it look like a sacrifice bunt). Just as the ball is released from the pitcher's hand, the batter rotates her body back about halfway (from her position to hit) while sliding her top hand back down the bat to a point just above the bottom hand. She brings both hands back and up to a point at about ear level so that when she takes a half swing at the ball, the plane of her swing is down through the ball so it goes down into the ground and not up into the air. (See figure 6.10.) The batter should hit the ball on the ground into either infield alley (see figure 6.11).

Drag Bunt

The drag bunt is used to surprise the defense. It may or may not be used with a runner on base. It is mainly designed to get the batter on base. The batter's intent is to get a good pitch and stay away from anything that isn't in the strike zone. Drag bunts are used by right- and left-handed batters and are executed differently in each case.

FIGURE 6.10
Slap bunt procedure.

Drag Bunt for a Right-Handed Batter

The batter begins with her normal batting stance. As the pitch is released from the pitcher's hand, the batter begins her move with simultaneous movements of her back foot and both hands. She takes a small step back from home plate with her rear foot and stays on the ball of this foot momentarily. As she steps back, she pulls the knob of the bat down and across her body with her bottom hand as her top hand slides up the bat to a position at the base of the barrel. The bat is brought out in front of the body, nearly parallel to the ground with the bottom hand along side the front hip. The batter then takes a small step with her front foot toward first base while bunting the ball to the ground a short distance from home plate (see figure 6.12).

Drag Bunt for a Left-Handed Batter

The left-handed batter also uses the drag bunt to surprise the defense. It may be used with a runner on base, but it is primarily used with the intent of getting the batter on base. Like the right-handed batter, the lefty is looking for a strike to bunt.

The batter begins with her normal batting stance. Just after the pitch is released, the batter takes a small step with her front foot and

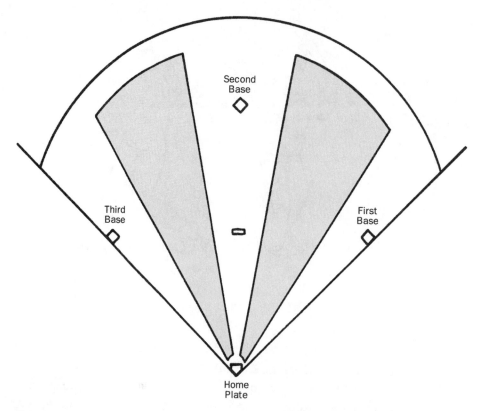

FIGURE 6.11
Infield alleys for slap bunt.

FIGURE 6.12
Sequence for the right-handed drag bunt.

places it directly under her own body to put herself in motion. This allows the back foot to cross over the foot that has been reset, and step toward the ball. She simultaneously pulls the bat down and across her body with her bottom hand as her top hand slides up the bat to the base of the barrel. The batter then levels the bat out in front of her body and bunts the ball a short distance in front of home plate (see figure 6.13).

BUNTING DRILLS

Catching the Ball with the Bat

Have the bunter take her normal batting stance. Have the tosser stand 6 to 8 feet in front of the batter. The tosser tosses the ball over the plate. The batter squares to sacrifice bunt the ball, and just before the ball contacts the bat, the batter lets go of the bat with the top hand (hang onto the bat with the bottom hand) and catches the ball with the top hand. This drill helps the batter with tracking skills and gives her the feel of keeping the barrel out to intercept the ball where it is pitched.

Directional Bunting

Put hula hoops on the ground about 4 to 5 feet in front of home plate along both baselines. Have a tosser or coach toss a ball to the batter who sacrifice bunts the ball so that the ball stops rolling inside a hula hoop. This drill helps the bunter learn to use bat angle to direct bunts down either baseline and helps her "give" with the ball, using the arms as shock absorbers. **Variations:** (1) Use a pitching machine to give the pitches greater velocity. (2) Adjust the hula hoops so that a push bunt will be necessary to get the ball in the hoop.

Squeeze Bunting

Set up a pitching machine on the mound and assemble a line of batters near home plate. Each batter gets one pitch to try to get the bunt down before going to the end of the line. Keep count of "good" bunts, and challenge your team to get five consecutive good ones down before you end the drill. **Variation:** Adjust the pitching machine slightly in between pitches to keep it game-like. Or, put runners at third base who lead off with the pitch and sprint toward home. Then switch lines to keep the drill going.

FIGURE 6.13
Sequence for the left-handed drag bunt.

HOW TO RUN THE BASES

It takes more than good speed to be a good baserunner. It takes a lot of brainpower as well. A good baserunner must always be aware of the count on the batter, the number of outs, the score and the inning, the coach's signals, and the locations of the defensive players. She must know the situation, be aware of her options, and be able to make quick decisions based on what is happening. This is also known as good "game sense."

All runners should know the basic mechanics of baserunning. Your players must understand how to run the bases in certain situations and be acquainted with the actions you want them to take and when it's safe to do so. Spend time with them to teach the proper lead off and whether you want the lead off to change from base to base. Drill your athletes on when to tag and when to draw the throw, and what each means. Have them check the playing depths of the outfielders prior to each pitch. Baserunning can be simple if athletes think about what they're going to do before the ball is ever hit. Teach athletes to preplan. When they don't think about what they're going to do ahead of time, they're liable to make poor choices and get themselves into some real jams.

Home to First

Running from home to first base includes four basic components—sneak a peak, run full speed through the base, look right, and break down.

1. **Sneak a Peak.** After the batter hits the ball and runs about 4 to 5 feet away from home plate, she takes a quick head check to look at the ball to see where it was hit.

2. **Run Full Speed.** The runner should run full speed toward first base in the running lane (see figure 6.14). If the coach is signaling the runner to run hard through the base, she should touch the front edge of the base with the foot that comes up

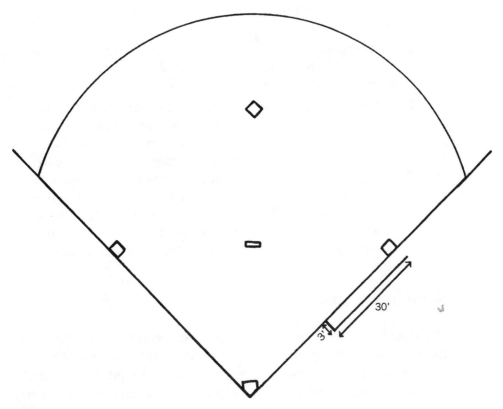

FIGURE 6.14
Softball infield showing the running lane to first base.

OVERRUNNING FIRST BASE

First base is the only base that a runner may overrun without the liability of being put out. If the runner overruns first base and turns to the right, she must return directly to first base. If the runner overruns first base and turns around to the left to head back to first base, she may either run to second base or return to first. Turning left to head back to first base is especially effective with teams that don't bother to cover second base on the play. If no one is covering, your runner may try to run to second base. If your runner turns left, however, and immediately heads for second base, then she must continue toward second. Check your rulebook for a specific explanation of this situation.

---

first and sprint through it with a few additional steps before slowing down.

3. **Look Right.** Immediately after crossing first base, the runner should look to her right, turning her entire head that way, searching for a possible overthrow on the play.

4. **Breakdown.** After crossing first base full speed, the runner should begin to brake by bending her knees and crouching slightly, as she slows to lower her center of gravity. If the baserunner sees the overthrow and can get to second base, she should use a reverse pivot (swinging her body open to home plate) with a driving step toward second base. If there is no overthrow, she should turn left, heading back to first base while keeping an eye on second base for the possibility of advancing if the defense forgets to cover second base.

Rounding a Base

The runner should round a base when she clearly has the base outright and needs to get into position to possibly advance to the next base, depending on what the defense does with the ball. When a baserunner rounds a base, she leans toward the infield and touches the inside corner of the bag with either foot (see figure 6.15). She should take three to four steps more and stop, crouching low with feet apart, to see if she can advance further or return to the bag previously touched.

FIGURE 6.15
Rounding the base.

Touching All the Bases

When the batter has an extra base hit, she will be touching more than one base. Figure 6.16 shows the correct path the runner should take when touching all the bases in order. The first base coach assists the runner with directions at first and second base while the third base coach assists the runner at second base and at third base until she reaches home.

Tagging Up on a Fly Ball

In fast-pitch softball, a runner may not advance on a fly ball until it is caught. With fewer than two outs, a runner who tags up on a fly ball has one foot on the base or bag, in a crouched position, ready to advance to the next base when the catch is made. It then becomes a race between the runner and the ball to get to the next base.

A runner may tag up on a fly ball and fake going to the next base. This is called, "drawing the throw." The runner tags up and

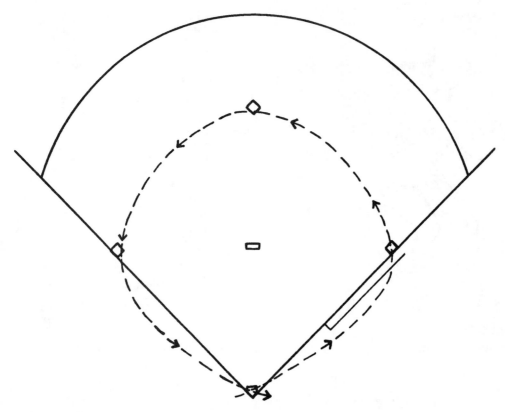

FIGURE 6.16
Correct path by baserunner when touching all bases.

sprints for three to five steps, only to stop and return to her bag. This strategy is commonly used by the offense when the ball hasn't been hit deep enough to allow the runner to advance, but the runner wants to force the defensive player to throw the ball anyway, to see if by chance she makes an errant throw.

Leading Off

When leading off of a base, the runner leaves the base when the ball leaves the pitcher's hand. If the baserunner is late getting a jump, she will be slow on the bases and will be a handicap for the offensive team. Use either the baseball style lead off or the momentum start at first and second bases. Use the walking lead at third base.

TIPS FOR THE BASERUNNER

1. Tag on a fly ball hit in the air behind you.

2. Go halfway on a fly ball hit in the air in front of you.

3. Freeze on a line drive.

4. Tag on any fly ball hit in foul territory.

5. On a ball that gets past the catcher, it's up to you to go. If you hesitate, get back!

6. On a ground ball hit to the pitcher, you freeze, unless forced.

7. On a ground ball on the infield ahead of you, freeze, unless forced.

8. When running to second base on a base hit into right field, look at the third base coach.

9. When running the bases, if there is an extra base hit in front of you, use your own judgment to decide how far to go. Use the third base coach only when necessary.

Baseball Style and Momentum Start Lead Off

The baseball style lead off is the most common and easiest to time with the pitcher's release point (see figure 6.17). The momentum start is more difficult to time with the pitcher's release point and takes more practice. The advantage to the momentum start is that because the runner is already moving prior to the pitch, she has a better jump on the ball once she leaves the bag (see figure 6.18). Using either lead off, the runner should take two to three steps to explode off the bag, and then square up to home plate briefly in a crouched position to see what the batter does with the pitch.

Walking Lead

I use the walking lead at third base only. I want the runner to stay under control (no explosion off the bag) and close to third base. We probably won't score on a ground ball on the infield anyway, so it's best to stay close to the bag to start. The runner begins with her left foot on the bag. On the pitch, she takes one crossover step with her left foot and then steps with her right foot to remain balanced while crouched. She doesn't explode, rather she walks these steps instead. If there's a base hit on a ground ball through the infield, she scores. If anything is hit into the air, she tags immediately and listens for

FIGURE 6.17
Sequence of baseball style lead off.

BASERUNNING DRILLS

Home to First

Have players line up at home plate. One at a time, they step to the plate and take a swing without the bat. They run to first base (sneak a peak, go full speed, hit the base, breakdown, look right) and turn left to head back to first while watching second. Then have the next player go. **Variation:** Place a coach in foul territory by first base with a ball. As the runner looks right, the coach either drops the ball to the ground or holds it. If the ball is dropped, the player executes a reverse pivot and goes to second. If the ball is not dropped, there is no overthrow and the player turns left and heads back to first.

All Bases

Put an equal number of players at all four bases. The first player at each base steps up, and only those runners execute the play together. The batter takes a swing without a bat and runs two bases, ending at second. She then jogs back to first base for her next turn. The runner at first goes on the swing and takes two bases, ending at third, then jogs back to second base. The runner at sec-

FIGURE 6.18
Sequence of momentum start.

ond goes on the swing, takes two bases, ending up at home plate, then jogs back to third base for her next turn. The runner at third, tags up on the swing, and scores. She remains at home and gets in line for her next turn. After the first group finishes, the next group steps up and repeats the drill.

LEAD OFF

Runners using the momentum start are notorious for getting a late jump. To help them, use two whistles—one for you and the other for another coach or player. Baserunners line up at first base. Put your pitcher and catcher in their positions. The first runner steps up and gets into position to lead off. Have your pitcher pitch the ball and tell the runner to go on the pitch and sprint out about 15 feet to simulate a steal. Blow your whistle when you see her foot leave the bag and have the other person blow his or her whistle when the ball leaves the pitcher's hand. If the runner is getting a perfect jump, both whistles should be heard together. If you get two separate whistle sounds, she's either leaving too late or too early.

PROGRESSION FOR TEACHING SLIDING

Day 1

Athletes should sit on the ground (preferably grass) with both legs extended straight out in front of them and hands in their laps. Tell them to keep the right leg straight and bend the left leg so that it lies on the ground on its side, with the left foot positioned just below the right knee. Have athletes lean back, almost lying on the ground, and raise both arms up and behind them into the air, with palms of the hands facing out. Explain that this is the correct body position when sliding feet first. Have them stand up. Announce that when you yell, "Get down!" you want them to drop to the correct sitting position for sliding feet first. Now yell, "Get down!" so that everyone can hear you. Make sure that they have all dropped into the correct body position (figure 6.19). Repeat this drill several times.

Day 2

Review the correct sitting position. Have athletes form a circle with at least two body lengths of distance between them. Have them all face in the same direction and begin walking around in a circle, maintaining the same distance between them. When you yell, "Get down!" they must drop to the correct sitting position for sliding feet first. Have them stay put until you can check their body positions. Do this several times until they drop into the proper sliding position consistently.

Day 3

Begin with a walk-through and yell "Get down!" for review. Then, with athletes in a circle, and with at least two body lengths of distance between them, have them go from walking to a slow jog. When you yell, "Get down!" they must drop to the correct sitting position for sliding feet first. Proceed as above. Repeat this drill several times until they get into the proper sliding position consistently from a slow jog. For each repetition of the drill, keep the formation the same but add more speed to the jogging. You don't want the athletes to get hurt.

FIGURE 6.19
Correct sliding position for the pop-up slide.

Day 4

When the athletes have mastered the skill to this point, take them to running full speed and sliding on a slip and slide. (This is especially fun when it's hot outside!)

Day 5

Place large pieces of cardboard in the baseline in front of the base. Make sure the athletes wear sweat pants or have their legs covered so they don't get burns from the cardboard. Your objective is to find ways to eliminate the fear of getting hurt associated with sliding. Have players start close to the base and jog toward the cardboard and slide from there if they like. Encourage them to start farther away and increase their jogging to a run when they can.

instructions. With this situation, I don't have to worry about the overaggressive runner who gets a huge lead down the third baseline on a line drive to the outfield, only to have to come back to tag after the catch is made and she is now unable to score. Had she been tagged up immediately, she would have scored on the play.

HOW TO SLIDE

Sliding into a base is one of the most difficult skills to teach in softball. This is not because the skill is so difficult, but because most young players fear that sliding is going to hurt. Your approach to sliding and the reassurance you give regarding players' comfort and safety will be the key to getting them to try it.

Introduce the following teaching progression gradually over a period of several days. Build your players' self-confidence and encourage them to try. You can't keep them from getting bumps and bruises in sports, but you can offer your support and guidance.

Although there are several ways to slide, the feet first pop-up slide will be the only one addressed in this section. Headfirst slides and hook slides are more advanced and should be taught to older players. Make sure your athletes are proficient at the pop-up slide before tackling more advanced techniques.

Work with your athletes on individual offensive skills. Many skills can be taught using stations where the athletes can work on one specific part of the larger skill in small groups while under the watchful eye of a coach. Hitting, bunting, baserunning, and sliding are all part of the action on offense, and when everybody can play a part in making the offense go, it can be great fun for all!

7

OFFENSIVE STRATEGIES IN TEAM PLAY

WHEN YOU UNDERSTAND individual offensive techniques in fast-pitch softball, you are ready to explore team play on offense. This consists of strategies or plays used to surprise the defense in an effort to help the batting team score runs. As the coach, you'll need to understand the individual abilities of your players and have signals to communicate with them. When your athletes are proficient in the individual skills on offense, they should be ready to combine their efforts as a team to execute plays and enhance the team's ability to score runs.

HOW TO USE OFFENSIVE TEAM STRATEGIES

Each offensive strategy is designed for use in a specific situation. The squeeze bunt, for example, is most effective when the runner on third has good speed and your batter is a good bunter. Suppose your best hitter is up to bat, and the defense is playing back at the corners (first and third base) because they expect the batter to hit away. You have less than two outs with runners at second and third bases respectively, and the runner at third has good speed. Your best hitter is also a good bunter, so you call the squeeze bunt, hoping to surprise the defense. As the pitcher releases the ball, the runner at third sprints home while your batter squares and lays down a beautiful bunt. The defense is late reacting to the bunt and cannot make a play on your runner who crosses home plate standing up. The defense recovers just in time to throw your batter out at first base. You survey the situation and realize that your team just scored a run, and you are threatening to score again because the baserunner that was at second moved to third on the play. Good job coach, you just made a great call! If you had tried to run the squeeze bunt with a slow runner at third or a poor bunter at the plate, your team's odds of successfully executing the play would have diminished dramatically. Certain elements need to be present in game situations to make it advantageous to run particular offensive plays.

Coaching Tip

Before your team plays its first game of the season, know which athletes are fastest. During practice, use a stopwatch to time your athletes on the bases. Record base running times from home to first, first to second, and second to home.

Because offensive strategies are designed for specific situations, you must be familiar with your athletes' strengths and weaknesses. Know which athletes are your better baserunners, because they have either exceptional speed or the ability to make smart decisions on the base paths. You should know which players are good bunters, and which are not. It may be time to use a particular team strategy in a game, but if you don't have the right athletes in the right places on offense, the probability of running the play successfully is lessened.

Table 7.1 shows eight basic team strategies, or plays, you can run on offense. Each strategy is shown with a list of the best conditions in which to use it, along with notes on how to execute the plays effectively. For example, the steal can be used anytime there is an open base ahead of a baserunner; however, there are conditions when a steal is more likely to be successful. Those conditions are listed under the column "Best to Use with." All of the listed conditions do not have to be present for the strategies to work effectively, but in general, the more conditions that are present, the better the chance of the play being successful. The column entitled "How to Execute" gives instructions on how to run the play for those athletes involved.

Table 7.1 The basic offensive team strategies, along with a list of what conditions are best suited for the plays and how to execute them

Offensive Strategy	Best to Use With	How to Execute
Bunt and Run	A batter that is a good bunter. A team where the defense keeps throwing the lead runner out on regular bunt plays. A slow runner on base.	Runner goes on the pitch, similar to a steal. Runner returns to base only if the ball is popped up. Batter must bunt next pitch (ball or strike).
Hit and Run	A runner at first base and a good contact hitter at bat. The batter ahead in the count (2-0, 3-1). A pitcher who is consistently around the plate. (This is difficult to execute with a wild pitcher.) A team that has been unsuccessful advancing runners with the bunting game.	Runner goes on the pitch, similar to a steal, however, she should look at the ball when it is hit to see where it goes. Runner should try for 2 bases on a base hit. Batter must hit the next pitch (ball or strike), preferably on the ground behind the runner. If the pitch is popped up, runner should return to the base.
Sacrifice Bunt	The score is close. Nobody out. A runner at first, second, or first and second.	Batter squares when pitcher's hands break apart. Bunt only strikes. Soft bunt, to make the defense have to throw to first for the out.
Squeeze Bunt	Less than 2 out, runners on second and third. A runner at third base having good speed. A batter who is a good bunter. The batter ahead in the count (3-0, 3-1, 2-0, 2-1).	Runner at third base goes on the pitch. Runner returns to base only if the ball is popped up. Batter squares upon pitcher's release. Batter must bunt next pitch (ball or strike).

(Continued)

Offensive Strategy	Best to Use With	How to Execute
Safety Squeeze	Less than 2 out, and a runner at third base.	Batter squares upon pitcher's release.
	A runner at third base having good speed.	Batter bunts only strikes.
	A batter who is a good bunter.	Runner does not go home on the pitch, but waits to see-
	The batter ahead in the count (3-1, 2-0, 2-1).	what the defense does with the ball.
Steal	A runner with an open base ahead.	Batter squares to fake sacrifice bunt, pulling bat away
	A runner having good speed.	from the ball as it enters the plate area.
	A catcher having a weak arm.	Runner goes on the pitch.
	An infielder not covering a base after the pitch.	
	2 out.	
Double Steal	Runners on first and second bases with good speed.	Batter squares to fake a sacrifice bunt, pulling bat away
	A catcher having a weak arm.	from the ball as it enters the plate area.
	An infielder not covering a base after the pitch.	Runners break upon pitcher's release and steal simulta-
		neously.
First and Third	Runners at first and third bases having good speed.	Batter squares when pitcher's hands break apart. Batter
	A catcher having a weak arm.	fakes a sacrifice bunt.
	The batter ahead in the count or early in the count.	Baserunner at first goes to second base upon pitcher's
		release and tries to steal second base. If the ball arrives
		at second base ahead of the runner, she should get
		caught in a rundown. If she can steal second base safely,
		she should do so.
		Runner at third base goes home if throw goes through to
		second base or at a strategic point on the ensuing rundown.

HOW TO COMMUNICATE THROUGH SIGNS AND SIGNALS

Offensive plays require signals, or signs that players and coaches give to each other by touching different parts of their bodies or clothing or some other action, that corresponds to a certain play or strategy. Give careful consideration to a signal system for your team. The age group of your athletes will likely dictate how many signals you have and how sophisticated they are. Develop signals for yourself and your athletes that are easy to see and understand.

The third base coach should give signals. The batter and all runners should look at the third base coach after every pitch to see if there is a signal for the ensuing pitch. You don't have to give signals prior to each and every pitch, but you should get in the habit of making touches between most pitches in an effort to keep the defense unsettled.

Signals should be easy to remember and easy to read. With younger players, use signals that create a mental connection or link between the sign and the skill. For example, touching the belt might correspond to the bunt, and touching skin might correspond to the steal. In each case, the first letter of the signal corresponds to the first letter of the skill.

The signals (play calling) should come from you, and athletes involved in the play should have a return sign. A return sign acknowledges that they have seen your signal and are prepared to execute the play you called. If you signal for the squeeze bunt, but only one player returns a sign, then you can assume the other player

MISSED HAND SIGNALS

Your players should have a hand signal for notifying you that they did not see your sign. That signal prompts you to quickly run through the signs again so that the players can see what is going on. I ask the players to roll their hands around each other at the waist, meaning "roll it again, coach." Also have your baserunners return the number of outs you flash to them. Too often, baserunners lose track of the number of outs and run the bases incorrectly. When you flash them "1 out," for example, with your index finger pointed to the sky, they should flash the same thing back to you. This technique keeps them constantly reminded of the number of outs.

doesn't know the play is on. Call a time-out before the next pitch is thrown to stop the play from occurring. This is vital in close games and can mean the difference between capitalizing on an offensive opportunity or throwing one away.

A baserunner might casually kick the bag or put her hands on her hips for a return sign. A batter might wipe down the bat or gently tap her shoes with the bat head before stepping into the batter's box to hit. The signs should be subtle and should not stand out from other types of actions for getting ready to play.

DRILLS

Signals

Have your athletes line up along the first baseline, spread out with an arm's length in between, and face you. Stand near the pitcher's mound. Tell your players they are at bat, and they are looking at you to get the signal. (Don't let them have bats at first; tell them to pretend they have bats.) Run through a series of signals and then have them pretend they are stepping into the batter's box to hit. Pretend to be the pitcher, and face home plate. Go through the pitching motion and watch to see if the players execute the correct action corresponding to the signal you gave. Did they give you a return sign before they stepped into the box? Did they do it correctly? Repeat the drill with another set of signals. **Variation:** Have athletes pretend they are baserunners at first base, and give signs for them to execute as a baserunner.

Small Diamond

Place a set of bases on the field at about 8 to 10 feet apart so that you have a small diamond. Position your players on defense and offense to work on specific situations without a bat or a ball. You will be able to keep the players close enough together to talk to all of them (without yelling because of the distances) to explain things and run more repetitions for timing and execution than if you were working at regulation distances. **Variation:** Use this teaching method at dusk when the light is fading and your players are unable to see the ball at practice. Bring them in closer with the small diamond and continue to work without bats and balls. This is ideal for teaching back-up coverages, position play on defense, and so forth.

Keep the number of signs to a minimum, regardless of your athletes' ages. The more signals you have, the more difficult they are to remember. Have signals for the basic plays and keep it simple. A good sacrifice bunt gets the job done whether the defense knows the play is coming or not. A well-executed play on offense is usually effective, even if the defense expects it.

Watching a fast-pitch softball team that executes well on offense is like watching a well-oiled machine at work. It performs flawlessly and, as a result, successfully. For the whole team to work effectively, team play on offense relies on the skills and abilities of individual team members. Coaches who are keenly aware of their athletes' proficiencies in certain softball skills and who know when conditions are right for implementing specific plays have a huge advantage over those who do not. A coach who can orchestrate all of this strategy with solid, simple two-way communication via signs and signals will create a team that is both fun to play on and fun to watch.

8

DEFENSIVE STRATEGIES IN TEAM PLAY

OFFENSE MAY WIN ball games, but it takes defense to stay in them. A team that can't play defense will get speedily blown out by a team that can. As is the case with offense, defensive strategies rely on the proficiency of each athlete's defensive skills and abilities. A catcher who throws erratically to second base negatively affects the team's success in trying to run the first and third situation on defense. It is therefore important to devote time to individual defensive skill development.

All fast-pitch teams should know what to do with the ball on defense. A team in any age group needs to learn where to throw the ball to get outs with runners in various positions on the bases. The transition game, relays, bunt defense, and double play are all basic lines of defense that your team should master as your athletes grow and develop. After mastering the basics, it becomes important to master more advanced defensive situations, such as the rundown and first and third plays.

HOW TO EXECUTE BASIC DEFENSIVE SITUATIONS

Athletes need to understand force plays and tag plays. A runner is forced to advance to the next base when all bases are occupied behind that runner, and the batter hits a fair ball on the ground, necessitating that she advance to first base. In this case, a force play may be made on any runner to get an out. A force out occurs when a defensive player touching a base is in possession of the ball before the runner reaches that base when she is forced to advance. For example, if there are runners at first and second bases with nobody out and the batter hits a ground ball to the pitcher, the runners are forced to advance to the next bases. If the pitcher fields the ball and throws it to the third baseman, who catches the ball and touches third base before the runner from second touches the bag, the runner is out on the force play and must return to the dugout. Now let's say the third baseman continues the play and throws to the second baseman, covering second base in an attempt to make the force play there as well. If the ball arrives ahead of the runner, the runner is forced out. If the runner arrives before the ball, she is safe and remains on the bag.

A tag play occurs when a fielder with the ball securely in her hand or glove touches a runner who is off the bag. When this occurs, the runner is out and must return to the dugout.

Defensive strategies used in situations with runners on base should focus on getting the lead runner out whenever possible. As its

FIELD TALK

Although tag plays may be made regardless of the situation, force plays require runners to be in certain positions on the bases. Encourage your players (infielders especially) to preplan and talk amongst themselves during games to help each other be more aware of the plays that exist on the infield. For example, if there are runners at first and second bases, your players should be saying things like, "Okay Jackie, we've got a force at third, be ready," or "Hey Mary, if she bunts, I've got first base." Situations change, and athletes need to learn to communicate this way on the field.

first priority, the defense should make an immediate play on the lead runner anytime she tries to advance to the next base (unless it's too late to make the play; in that case, the play should be redirected to get the out at first base). The lead runner, however, won't always advance if she's not forced. This is certainly the case when a ground ball is fielded quickly by the defense, and the runner may not feel she has the speed to advance safely. Instead of advancing, she takes a leadoff and waits to see what happens with the play.

Figure 8.1 shows the various situations in which infielders on defense might find themselves and the corresponding strategies to use when making a play on a ground ball. For example, if there is a runner at second base with only one out, an infielder should field the ground ball first, then hold the runner (look at her intently as if to make the play on her), and get the out at first base. With bases loaded and two outs, the object is to make a play on the runner that is the easiest out to make, or throw to first for the routine ground ball out. The shortstop may field the ball in the baseline and reach out to tag the runner advancing to third base to complete the easiest out on a nearby runner.

The defensive positioning of infielders doesn't change much unless there is a runner on third base with less than two outs. In this situation, the infield shortens up, with the corners moving in a few steps and the middle infielders taking positions just inside the

| | | **SITUATIONS BY NUMBER OF OUTS** | |
		Less Than 2 Out	2 Out
SITUATIONS BY WHETHER OR NOT FORCE EXISTS ON LEAD RUNNER	**Force Exists**	Make the play on the lead runner	Make the play on the runner who is the easiest out, or get the out at first base.
	Force Does Not Exist	Hold the lead runner and get the out at first	

FIGURE 8.1

Various situations and corresponding ground ball plays for infielders to make on defense.

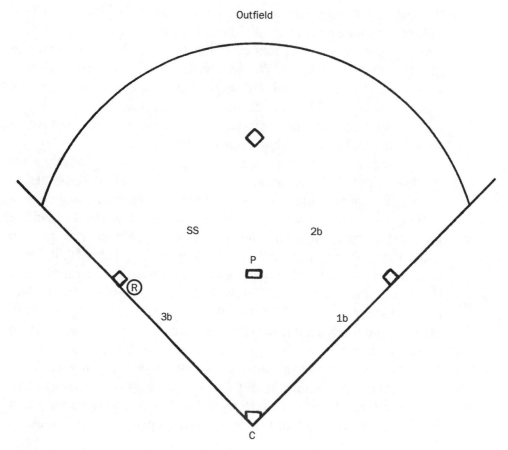

FIGURE 8.2
Infield starting positions with the lead runner on third base with less than two outs.

baselines. This positioning shortens the distance they will have to throw in making the play at home plate in time for the out (see figure 8.2).

HOW TO RUN THE TRANSITION GAME

The transition game on defense refers to how the infielders and outfielders work together to handle balls hit into the outfield with runners on base. Outfielders may throw to teammates who are "cut-off" players, or they may be involved on longer plays requiring teammates to relay the ball to home plate. It is a cardinal sin for an outfielder to hold a ball in the outfield. Outfielders should quickly field the ball and know where to throw it on the infield. Communication from adjacent teammates in the outfield is crucial to helping a teammate know where to throw.

Coaching Tip

Encourage outfielders to talk to the teammate making the play. Adjacent outfielders can see what is developing on the infield with regard to runners and can tell the fielder where to throw. Simply saying, "Throw to Janie!" can save time and indecision.

Just as in infield play, the focus from the outfield is on the lead runner. If a batter hits a single with nobody on, the outfielder should throw to second base. Get your outfielders thinking that they need to throw two bases ahead of where the lead runner starts on a simple base hit. This is another great reason to preplan before the ball is ever hit. If the batter gets a single with a runner on first base, the throw from the outfield should go to third base (two bases ahead of where the runner started).

With runners in scoring position (e.g., second and third base), a base hit to the outfield can usually score a run. Therefore, it is critical that an outfielder fields the ball as quickly as possible and comes up throwing to home plate. From that point, it is incumbent upon the infielders to position themselves strategically for various plays based on what the base runners do. This exchange of the ball from the outfield to the infield is the transition game.

How to Run the Cut-Off

Infielders have different responsibilities as the ball transitions from the outfield to the infield. When a runner tries to score on a ball hit to the outfield, a cut-off is established on the infield for the throw to home plate. It is the cut-off player's job to be in direct line with the throw to home from the outfield and to cut the ball off or stop it from reaching home plate when told to do so by the catcher. The ball is cut:

1.   When the throw is too late to get the runner out at home plate and there are other runners on base. This prevents the ball from getting by the catcher and allowing runners to advance further.

2.   When the lead runner stops at third base and there is no play at home. This prevents the ball from getting by the catcher and allowing runners to advance further.

3.   When the throw is too late to get the runner out at home plate but there is still time to make a play on another runner. The ball doesn't have to go all the way through to the catcher but can instead be intercepted sooner to make the out on a trail baserunner.

The catcher makes all cut-off calls, including those that redirect the play to another base. Figure 8.3 shows the location of the cut-off position on the infield. Generally, the position is taken somewhere along a line of the pitcher's mound running foul line to foul line.

Three different players share cut-off responsibilities. The first baseman is the cut-off on most throws to home with a runner in scoring position. The third baseman becomes the cut-off when the ball is hit on the ground in the 5-6 hole and goes through into the outfield. The first baseman must cover first base if the shortstop makes the backhand play on the grounder. Once the ball goes through to the outfield, it is much easier for the third baseman to move into the cut-off position on that side of the field while the shortstop covers third base. The pitcher is the cut-off on the short one-hop base hit into right field. The first baseman must cover first base to give the right fielder a chance to throw out the batter/base runner. But if the outfielder elects to throw home instead, the pitcher is in position to be the cut-off.

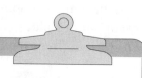

Coaching Tip

If your right fielder has a very weak arm, move your cut-off player away from home plate to get the ball sooner. These types of adjustments may be made on almost any type of positioning.

How to Run the Relay

There are times when an outfielder has to run down a well hit ball and use a relay player to get the ball back to the infield. Middle infielders usually play

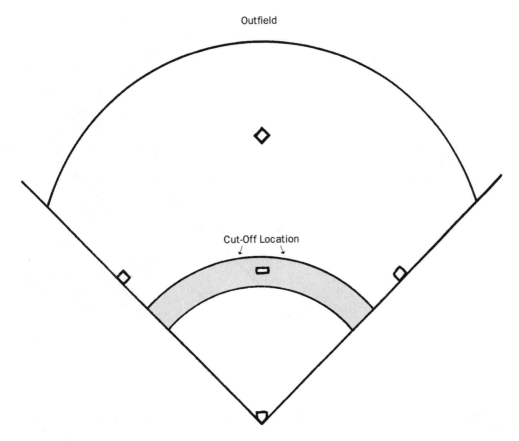

FIGURE 8.3
Diagram of the location for the cut-off player on the infield.

the role of the relay player because of their closer proximity to out-fielders. The shortstop generally relays long balls hit to the left fielder and center fielder. It is the second baseman's responsibility to relay long balls hit to the right fielder. Figure 8.4 shows the relative positions of the relay players on the field.

The relay player should catch and release the ball as soon as possible, receiving the throw from the outfielder in the air and on the glove side of the body. To catch the ball in the air, she must adjust the distance she travels onto the outfield grass based upon the arm

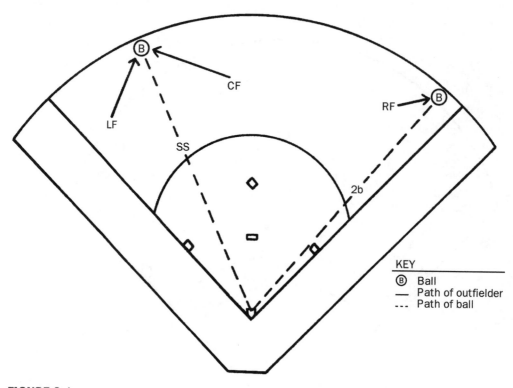

FIGURE 8.4

The shortstop and second baseman in correct relay positions for long balls hit to two different locations in the outfield.

strength of her outfielder teammate. If the outfielder's arm is weak, the relay player will have to go out farther than for an outfielder with a stronger arm. The key is to avoid any short hop the ball might take prior to reaching the relay player. Figure 8.5 shows the correct body position for taking the throw from the outfielder and transitioning into the throw to the infield.

HOW TO EXECUTE THE BUNT DEFENSE

From a defensive standpoint, the goal of the bunt defense is to get the lead runner out whenever possible, but to always end up making an out on the play. And often it means getting the batter out at first base. An aggressive bunt defense that constantly foils the attempts

FIGURE 8.5
Sequence of the correct body position of the relay player taking the outfield throw and transitioning into the throw to the infield.

by the offense to advance runners can be highly effective in shutting down the opposition.

Your primary fielders are the four infielders closest to the ball. Figure 8.6 shows the basic coverage areas of those four infielders—pitcher, catcher, first baseman, and third baseman. The shortstop and second baseman are responsible for covering specific bases.

When the ball is bunted, all four infielders charge in to field the ball. The player who gets to the ball first calls for the ball and fields it. It is the catcher's responsibility to call out the base to which the fielder will throw. Since the catcher can see the entire infield and also monitor the baserunner's position on the base path at the time the bunt is fielded, she directs the flow of the play. If there is indecision on the play, or if the player fielding the bunt does not hear the catcher's call, then she should automatically throw to first base to get the batter out.

The offensive team may choose to bunt in a variety of situations. Base coverage responsibilities change depending on where the runners are positioned at the time of the bunt. Figure 8.7 shows all possible positions of baserunners and the corresponding assignment of those players covering the bases. On a bunt with runners at first and second

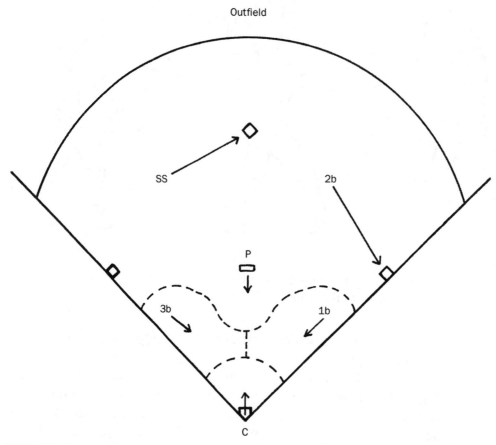

FIGURE 8.6
Basic bunt coverage areas of the pitcher, catcher, first baseman, and third baseman. Also shown are the middle infielders and the bases they cover on the bunt with a runner at first base.

bases, the shortstop covers third base, the second baseman covers first base, and the catcher covers home plate. Second base is left open, or the center fielder may move in to show that second base is covered; however, the infielders should be careful about making a play at that base. Remember, it is the job of the pitcher, catcher, first baseman, and third baseman to field any bunt in their territory first, and then drop back to cover their respective bases accordingly.

BASE TO BE COVERED

	Home	First	Second	Third
1st	Catcher (P)*	2nd Baseman	Shortstop	3rd Baseman (C)*
2nd	Catcher	2nd Baseman	Leave Open**	Shortstop
3rd	Catcher	2nd Baseman	Leave Open**	Shortstop
1st & 2nd	Catcher	2nd Baseman	Leave Open**	Shortstop
1st & 3rd	Catcher	2nd Baseman	Leave Open**	Shortstop
2nd & 3rd	Catcher	2nd Baseman	Leave Open**	Shortstop
1st, 2nd, & 3rd	Catcher	2nd Baseman	Leave Open**	Shortstop

POSITION OF RUNNERS

*If the third baseman fields the bunt, then the catcher covers third base until the third baseman can return to cover her bag. Likewise, the pitcher covers home plate until the catcher returns.

**Leave second base open, or uncovered. Another option would be to bring the center fielder in to show coverage of the bag, but the infielders should be cautioned against making a play at second base because there will be no outfielder backing up the play.

FIGURE 8.7

Various positions of baserunners and the infielders assigned to cover each base on the bunt.

DEFENDING THE SLAP BUNT

When defending the slap bunt, the defense must change its strategy. Obviously, you won't know beforehand that the batter is going to slap bunt—that's what makes it so effective. When the batter squares to bunt, your corners must charge in to play the bunt, but your middle infielders must hold their positions until they are sure the ball is on the ground for a bunt. If the batter squares and then pulls her bat back to slap bunt, everyone that sees it should yell, "Slap!" and your charging corners should brake to a stop and pinch the alleys, or take a few quick steps in toward the pitcher. The slap bunt is then handled like a ground ball, and the other infielders take on the responsibilities they would normally have on a ground ball.

HOW TO EXECUTE THE DOUBLE PLAY

The double play is one of the most beautifully executed plays on defense. There is something special about the speed, timing, and physical ability needed by an infielder to execute a play that results in the elimination of two baserunners in such rapid succession. The double play is rather common in baseball because of the greater distances involved between bases. Fast-pitch softball has its share of double plays, but because the bases are much closer together, the double play is more of a rare treat, and must be executed with real efficiency. The initial throw to second base, the footwork on the pivot, and the throw to first base must all be free of wasted time and motion for it to work effectively. Because the ball changes hands several times, it takes practice working together to get it just right.

The Initial Throw

The initial throw on the double play must be made efficiently. Great care must be taken not to take any unnecessary steps or waste time

DOUBLE PLAY

Talk with infielders about the proper mindset needed to turn a double play. It's a tough play to run, and what is most important is getting the out at second base. If you get the out at first base, consider it a bonus on the play. Too often double plays are botched early on because all the players are focused on hurrying because of the close play at first base. As a result, the initial throw to second base is bad or the pivot player drops the ball. Each player has a small role in the larger double play, and each should learn to focus on the execution of her task only. When the third baseman fields the ground ball, she should only think of making a timely, chest-high throw to second base. She needs to let the pivot player worry about the necessary footwork at second base and throwing to first base in time. When the third baseman fields the ball and thinks that she has to hurry up and throw to second because of the close play at first base, she is actually focusing on first base instead of on what she needs to think about—the throw to second base!

in making the throw to second base. Middle infielders must work to get to the ball quickly and field it on the midline of the body whenever possible. When the shortstop fields the ball on the midline, she should leave her right foot planted as she fields the ball and simply take one step with the left foot to make a side-arm throw to second base. The second baseman should also field the ball on the midline of the body whenever possible, and then either rotate only her upper body to make the throw, or pivot on her right foot to step with the left foot to make the throw. An extra step saved on the initial throw to second base may mean the difference between getting the runner out at first base by a step or missing the out by a step.

The Pivot

Efficiency and quickness in executing the pivot at second base are the goals of the middle infielder. It is the middle infielder's job to receive the initial throw and secure the out at second base. She must then maneuver off the bag and make a strong throw to first base to complete the double play.

The Shortstop's Pivot

The shortstop should use either of two different pivots, depending upon where the initial throw originates. Any throw originating from a position inside the baseline between first base and second base should be taken on the inside of the bag. Any throw taken outside of that same baseline should be taken on the back corner of the bag.

The footwork for a throw taken on the inside of the base is slightly different from the footwork used for a throw on the back corner of the bag. Figure 8.8 shows the correct footwork on the inside of the bag. After the catch is made, the shortstop pivots on the right foot and takes only one step toward first base to make the throw. The fewer steps that are taken, the better the odds are of getting the batter out at first base. (For figures 8.8–8.11, the foot patterns indicate the locations of the steps taken, and the numbers indicate their proper sequence.)

The footwork on the back corner of the bag requires a few additional steps to get the shortstop in position to make the throw. Figure 8.9 shows the correct footwork for a throw originating from outside the baseline. After receiving the throw, the shortstop drags her right foot across the top of the back corner of the bag and steps to a position just behind the vacating left foot as it steps toward first base for the throw to complete the double play.

The Second Baseman's Pivot

The second baseman can use two different pivots at second base. The decision to use either technique is a matter of personal choice. Figure 8.10 shows the pivot most commonly used. It allows the second baseman to stay behind the bag when making the throw to first base. Figure 8.11 shows another technique that involves the second baseman crossing over the bag and throwing to first from a position in front of second base.

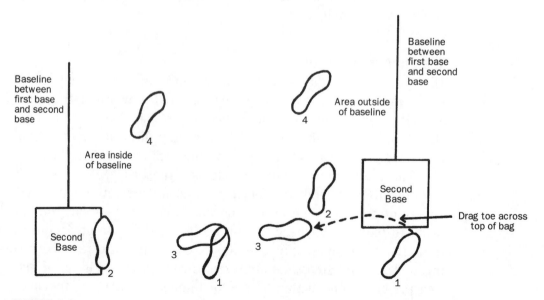

FIGURE 8.8
Correct footwork used by the shortstop on the double play pivot when taking a throw originating from inside the baseline.

FIGURE 8.9
Correct footwork used by the shortstop on the double play pivot when taking a throw originating from outside the baseline.

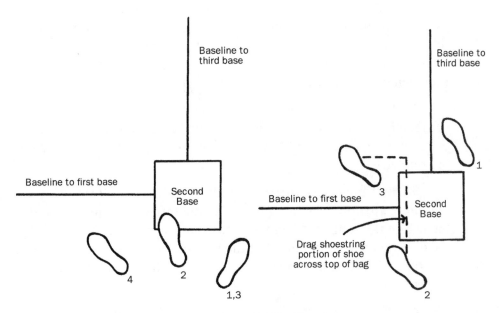

FIGURE 8.10
Second baseman's pivot with a throw to first from behind the bag. The actual catch should be made on step 2.

FIGURE 8.11
Second baseman's pivot moving forward across the bag. Note that step 2 is taken by dragging the top of the shoe (shoestring portion) across the bag and then stepping directly toward first base to make the throw. The actual catch should be made on step 1.

HOW TO EXECUTE THE RUNDOWN

The rundown is a more advanced defensive team strategy that involves putting out a runner trapped between bases. Baserunners may get caught off base for a variety of reasons and may suddenly find themselves scrambling to find the nearest open base. Because rundowns occur between bases, infielders should be trained to handle the ball in these situations.

The object of the rundown is to get the runner out using the fewest number of throws between infielders as possible. I have devised a set of rules that all infielders should follow to make executing the rundown a little easier.

1. Run the baserunner back to the base she is coming from. For example, if the runner is caught between third base and home, the infielder should run the baserunner back toward third base. If more than one throw is necessary, every attempt must be made to keep the rundown operating nearest third base.

2. Show the ball. The infielder should keep the ball visible to her teammates at all times, holding the ball in the quick-snap throw position until she is ready to either throw the ball or make the tag on the runner.

3. Run full speed. Infielders must learn to run full speed at the runner, to convince the runner that the infielder is going to put the tag on the runner. When the baserunner turns her head to face in the direction she is running (i.e., the infielder can see the back of the baserunner's helmet), then the baserunner has turned to go full speed.

4. Use a snap throw. Do not wind up to throw. If the infielder is running full speed, the momentum she is generating is sufficient to use the snap throw. Otherwise, she'll throw the ball too hard to a teammate.

5. Close the gap. An infielder covering the base that was last touched by the baserunner should hold her position at the bag. As the rundown moves back toward the base the runner is coming from, the waiting infielder at the next base should close the gap or distance on the rundown. For example, if the runner is being run back to first base, the second baseman should move about 20 feet (one-third the distance) closer to first base while remaining in the base path. Then, if the runner is able to turn and run back toward second base, the defense can narrow the field to help contain the runner better.

6. Follow the throw. An infielder should follow her throw to a teammate to replace the person she just threw to. This ensures that there is always a player filling a spot that a teammate has just vacated in case the rundown comes back to that spot.

7. Tag the runner with the ball in the glove. Protect the ball on the tag. Barehanded tags made with the ball in the throwing hand can easily come loose and result in a dropped ball.

Infielders need to judge when to throw the ball to a teammate in a rundown. This good judgment only comes with practice. An infielder must learn to recognize speed, closing distance, and the positions of teammates in a rundown so that she can throw the ball to a teammate in time to make the tag on a runner. An infielder can yell, "Ball," if she feels the timing is right for her teammate to throw her the ball. If the ball is held too long, the runner is likely to run past the waiting fielder and end up safe at the bag. Figure 8.12 shows

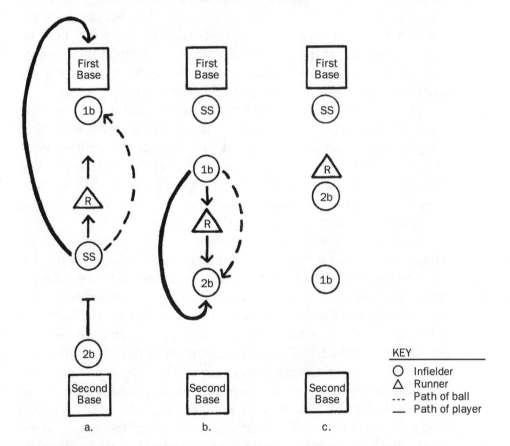

FIGURE 8.12
Rundown between first and second bases in three different stages. (a) The shortstop runs the baserunner back toward first base and then follows her throw, or replaces the first baseman after she throws the ball. The second baseman closes the gap. (b) The first baseman runs the baserunner toward second base and then follows her throw. The shortstop remains at the bag. (c) The second baseman makes the tag on the baserunner.

three stages of a rundown between first and second bases. The runner should be tagged at any point and as soon as possible.

HOW TO EXECUTE THE FIRST AND THIRD PLAY

The first and third play is the most difficult and, therefore, the most advanced play to make on defense. It is introduced here for those teams and players who are advanced enough to be able to manage it. A prerequisite to knowing how to execute the first and third play is proficient execution of the rundown. The first and third play is like a double rundown. Runners at first and third bases move freely in their respective base paths at the same time. Although it's tricky to run, there are modifications for executing the play. Either way, it takes practice.

The basic play begins with runners on first and third bases. The goal of the offensive team is to get the defense so involved in making a play on the runner stealing second base that the runner from third base scores. If that doesn't work, the runner at first base can safely steal second base, giving the offense two runners in scoring positions. It is the goal of the defense, then, to put out the runner stealing second while keeping the runner at third base from scoring.

When the runner at first base tries to steal second base, the defense moves into a defensive alignment designed specifically for this play (see figure 8.13). The catcher throws down to second base on the steal (she quickly checks to see that the baserunner at third is not sprinting home as she winds up to throw). The second baseman moves to a position between the pitcher's mound and second base and may cut off the ball if she sees the runner at third base break for home. If the runner at third doesn't move, the second baseman lets the throw go through to the shortstop covering second base. If the runner going to second stops before reaching the base and gets caught in a rundown, the shortstop should run the runner back toward first base, thus beginning the rundown. The second baseman should fill in at second base.

The runner at third base may break for home at any time. It is the job of the third baseman to keep the infielders apprised of various things the third-base runner is doing. For example, if the runner takes a lead off and then stops and waits, the third baseman yells, "Holding! Holding!" If the runner breaks for home, she yells, "Going!

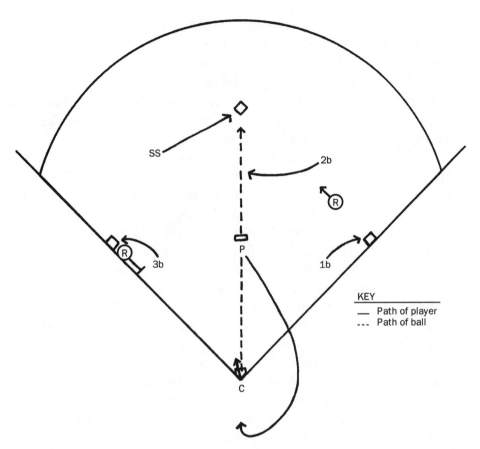

FIGURE 8.13
The infielders and their positioning when executing the first and third play.

Going!" If the runner gets a good distance off third base, she yells, "Take a look! Take a look!" Infielders executing the rundown between first and second bases may play on the runner at third when they have a chance to put her out. If they get the runner at third caught in a rundown, the infielders then forget the runner between first and second bases and focus their collective efforts on the new rundown developed between home and third base.

First and Third Play Modifications

There are several modifications to the first and third play that may make the play easier to run. The first modification is sort of a relay down to second base on the steal. When the runner at first base breaks for second, the catcher immediately throws the ball back to the pitcher, who turns toward the runner at third base and then throws to second base to get the runner stealing. If the runner going to second stops and gets caught in a rundown, then the shortstop begins the rundown between first and second while monitoring the runner at third. The rest of the play continues as described previously.

The second modification involves a complete slowdown of the play by the shortstop. If the runner at first base tries to steal second, then the catcher throws down, first checking the runner at third, as in the original play. If the runner heading toward second stops and gets caught in a rundown, the shortstop takes the ball and walks toward first base while head checking at third and walking step by step toward first base. The baserunner between first and second will likely walk as well. The shortstop slowly closes the gap and tries to nip the runner out at first base in the end. If the runner returns safely to first base and the other runner remains at third, then the defense should ask the umpire for a time-out to hold the runners, thus ending the play.

Team defense requires every player to know what to do with the ball in a variety of situations and the importance of working together with teammates. Drill your team on the basics and gradually work toward more advanced strategies. Situations involving baserunners should be a part of nearly every practice. It is through repetition and practice that your players begin to execute plays on defense with good judgment and confidence. When your athletes play solid defense, you'll find your team in every ball game.

9

PLANNING FOR THE SEASON

TO PLAN FOR the season, you need to be an architect of sorts. You have to have a vision of what you want the product (team) to look like, and then you have to design the plans for how you're going to build it. The design phase is critical—make a mistake here and you may not get what you'd hoped for. For you and your athletes to get the most out of your upcoming season, commit time and energy in the beginning to carefully plan the year in advance.

You'll want to begin your planning for the season with a calendar. After you've logged all game dates, practice days, meetings, and all other team-related functions, you'll have a pretty good lay out with which to work. Now it's up to you to fill in the blanks. How many practice opportunities will you have to get your athletes ready for your first game? How will you get them ready for your first game? How proficient are they now? What do they need to learn? How in the world do you get to there from here? To find the answers, let's first step away from the bigger picture and focus on a few smaller pieces—pieces that when finally put back together, help create the complete picture of a properly prepared team.

A successful plan for a season contains several elements. First of all, goal setting is paramount. You need to know what it is you want to accomplish before you can chart a course for getting there. Also, establishing a positive tone with parents and players at the beginning of the season is essential for a smooth running organization. Parents can be your greatest allies or your worst nightmares. Taking some simple steps at the start of the season can help get them on your side early. Finally, practice planning that has been guided by solid goal setting is important to help you stay the course and keep on track. Planning the right practices will properly prepare your team for games, and because game days can often be a bit chaotic, you'll want to make game days as easy for you to enjoy as you can.

HOW TO SET GOALS

Goals are important because they give us direction in life; they point us toward the end result of what it is we want. If we didn't have any goals, we'd probably just wander around and be pretty unproductive. It is up to us to come up with a plan to achieve or attain that end result. This plan had better be pretty accurate, or we're going to waste an awful lot of valuable time and effort. That's why it's sometimes helpful to have other goals, or sub-goals, along the way. Sub-goals can help to keep us on the right track.

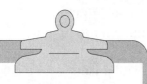

Coaching Tip

Be careful about establishing goals that involve winning. Success isn't always measured by winning. Focus on individual parts of the game, such as the team's ability to bunt successfully. This focuses the team on the fundamentals, which, when mastered on a consistent basis, will lead to winning.

You set goals for a softball season in much the same way that you would set goals for a long road-trip or a trek up Mount Everest. You have main goals and sub-goals for what you want to accomplish with your team. These goals will help you to formulate your plan for the season. The important thing is to make your goals attainable, or realistic. Unrealistic goals are a set-up for disappointment. If you set your team up for unrealistic goals, and then subsequently plan for failure, the results can be devastating for young athletes, especially in areas where self esteem and self-confidence may already be lacking. Take time to set-up realistic goals and formulate a plan for success. The experience will be very rewarding for both you as a coach and your kids.

You may elect to set goals for the coaching staff, goals for the parents, and goals for your athletes. Be sure to allow those individuals input into the goal-setting process. This is a good idea for several reasons. First, you will likely gain some insight into what is viewed as realistic and what is not. There's more at stake here then just your perception of what the group can realistically do. You might, for example, find your coaches setting their sights even higher than yours. Second, those persons giving input will be more likely to want to achieve the goals that are established. If they feel they played a role in helping to set the course for the group, then they'll be more likely to want to see the goals achieved.

Often, goal setting for softball teams revolves mainly around performance. You have probably seen or heard of high profile coaches and players who vow to win titles and championships at year's end. But winning isn't everything. Therefore, it is a good idea for you to include goals pertaining to the behavioral expectations that you have of your young people, especially because you will be responsible for some of their personal and social development. Goals pertaining to things like sportsmanship and behavior toward coaches and teammates are important avenues of development when coaching the young female athlete.

Goals may be either qualitative or quantitative in nature. The box titled Behavioral Goals for Your Players lists examples of qualitative goals. That is, the goals refer to a certain quality or qualities of behavior in individuals. A quantitative goal, on the other hand, refers to an amount or some number of something, for example, batting .300 for the season. The nice thing about quantitative goals is that they are measurable, and it is easy to determine whether or not

---

BEHAVIORAL GOALS FOR YOUR PLAYERS

Because you are responsible for part of the personal and social development of your players, it is a good idea to implement behavioral goals. Some examples of appropriate behavioral goals are:

1. to show support and encouragement of teammates during games, practices, and all other team functions

2. to be clean and neat in appearance while representing the team during games, practices, road trips, and other team functions

3. to show good sportsmanship toward opponents

someone has attained their goal. Qualitative goals, however, are more difficult to measure and therefore difficult to assess in terms of success or failure. I may be well intended in setting a goal of wanting my team to have fun over the course of the season, but I will have a hard time measuring and assessing this goal at the end of the year. Did my players have fun? Although I could ask them, they might not all agree on whether they had any fun at all!

Prior to the start of the season, write a list of general goals for the coaching staff (and parents too if you feel it is necessary). Keep the goals simple and don't have too many. Three or four goals for the coaching staff are plenty. When you meet with your staff, ask them for input into the goal setting process. Share with them what goals you think are important, and ask for feedback. Discuss the pros and cons of the different goals and then agree to three or four main goals for the coaching staff. Once you have settled on the goals, write them down and give each member a copy.

It is difficult to establish real team goals until you've had a chance to evaluate your team. To determine what you want to accomplish with your team, you first need to find out where your team is in terms of skills and abilities. When you first meet as a group, watch your team perform the basic skills, such as throwing, catching, fielding, batting, bunting, and base running. Try to assess their individual abilities and overall ability as a team. How much work do you expect to have to do with them? If you're like most coaches, the answer is a lot! Don't get overwhelmed at this point, just take it one step at a time.

Solid fundamental play is the most important part of the game. Evaluate your team and evaluate and list the basic things your team does fairly well and what needs work (see table 9.1). This list will serve as a starting point and will help you plan your practices. Throughout the season, you'll continue to work on what the team does well, but you'll also focus on what needs work. As you spend more time with your team in practice, you'll be able to determine more specific needs of your individual athletes as well. Continue to jot down notes and keep files on your players. The information that you gather will help you develop a profile of your team's skill level. This will then enable you to develop and plan productive practices.

Coaching Tip

Typical goals for your staff might include making sure that each staff member provides some type of instruction to each athlete at every practice or that each member says something positive to each player at each practice.

Table 9.1 Sample team evaluation chart.

THE WHIZ KIDZ
TEAM EVALUATION

Date: _____

Time: _____

Location: _____

RATING: 1 = Below Average; 2 = Average; 3 = Above Average

PLAYER/POSITION	SKILL				
	Throwing	Catching	Fielding	Batting	Base running
Tami Thacher/C	3	3	3	2	3
Taz Berry/SS	3	3	2	3	2
Karly Sue/P	2	2	2	2	2
Weezer Lala/3b	3	3	2	1	2
Jackie Michael/1b	3	2	2	1	2
Clarise Shannon/OF	1	2	2	2	3
Bailey Johnsen/2b	2	2	2	1	3
Hailey Foster/OF	3	3	2	2	2
Andi Renee/OF	1	2	2	2	2
Erin Lisa/P	3	3	2	3	2

Notes: Group needs to work on hitting; slow bat speed and poor command of the strike zone. Fielding is weak; players could benefit from lots of repetition and fielding drills, some unsure of where to throw the ball. Throwing and catching skills seem strong so that is a good base from which to work. The group is lively and several girls have played together before.

Once the team evaluation is complete, you'll be ready to establish general performance goals for your players. Use the areas of weakness that you have identified in your team evaluation to help you set goals (see table 9.2). Try to be as specific as possible in setting performance goals. Establish sub-goals to help keep you on course. Think of sub-goals as a day-to-day approach that will help you accomplish larger goals that may take many weeks. You can also use this same procedure to further evaluate and develop goals for individual athletes as well.

Table 9.2   Sample performance goal plan.

WHIZ KIDZ
PERFORMANCE GOALS

Date: _____

1. To have every athlete compete in every game. **(General Goal)**

    (sub-goals)

    a. To devise a list of all players and the positions they are proficient in to have at every game.

    b. To rotate starting line-ups game to game so that every player has a chance to start at least once during the season.

    c. To develop a record of all the players and the number of innings played in each game.

2. To improve individual fielding skills over the course of the season. **(General Goal)**

    (sub-goals)

    a. To spend 10 minutes of each practice in small groups fielding grounders and flies.

    b. Introduce a new defensive drill at each practice.

    c. Introduce a new defensive competitive challenge drill at every other practice.

3. _____ **(General Goal)**

    (sub-goals)

    a. _____

    b. _____

    c. _____

4. _____ **(General Goal)**

    (sub-goals)

    a. _____

    b. _____

    c. _____

HOW TO CONDUCT A PARENT MEETING

The degree of involvement by some parents in youth sports is causing educators, coaches, and administrators of youth sports programs in this country a great deal of concern. Coaches need to understand that as long as there are youth sports there will be parents close at hand. Consequently, it is in your best interest as a coach to educate and communicate with parents very early in the process, before your first game or practice ever begins. Take the time to conduct a parent meeting. You can even choose to include your athletes in this meeting. Chapter 2 outlines the steps to take in conducting such a meeting and what your agenda should include. I won't be redundant here in repeating any information, only to make the point that a parent meeting should be a part of the planning process for the upcoming season.

Coaching Tip

Learning occurs in the brain, not the muscles. If a player repeats a skill too often at one time, the muscles will tire and performance will deteriorate, often causing athletes to learn bad habits to compensate for poor performance. Reduce the numbers of repetitions to get quality practice.

HOW TO PLAN PRACTICE

Practice is the time when you and your athletes work together to improve various softball skills, through drills and related activities, so that the team can effectively play a game of softball. And if you're like most coaches, there never seems to be enough time to accomplish everything you'd like to achieve in one practice. But it's all the time you have, and you'd better take advantage of every second with your players. Your first game is fast approaching, and you want your players to look good on the field. After all, it will be a reflection of how well you have prepared them! Do you know everything that they'll need to know?

At the start of the season, it can be very helpful to compile a comprehensive list of all the things your players need to know to play a game of softball. You can make up your own list, or you can adjust the one provided in table 9.3 to fit your own team needs. Use this list to help you plan your practices and make sure you practice what you need to know for the first game.

You may not be able to teach your athletes everything they need to know about the game of softball prior to your first game. Rather than being overwhelmed by the brevity of it all, prioritize your list,

Table 9.3 Sample list of softball basics and knowledge for coaches and players

BASIC SKILLS AND ABILITIES OF SOFTBALL

Individual Defensive Skills/Abilities

Throwing

Catching

Fielding grounders

Fielding flies

Catches in the sun

Tagging runners

Making/understanding force outs

Rules knowledge

Team Defense

Situations, coverages

Transition play/Relays & cut-offs

Bunt, slap, squeeze

Double play

Rundowns

1st & 3rd situation

Right of way with pop-ups/flies

Steal

Backing up bases

Individual Offensive Skills/Abilities

Hitting

Bunting, slapping, squeeze bunt

Base running

Sliding

Tagging up

Drawing the throw

Stealing

Taking signals

Rules knowledge

Team Offense

Hit and run

Bunt and run

1st & 3rd situation

Double steal

Squeeze

beginning with the basics. Save the more complex or sophisticated team strategies for later, when they're ready. You can be sure you won't be the only team in this situation. So use your goals to guide you, and you'll be on your way!

Planning Practice

Planning practice is one of the most important things you will do as a coach. Try to establish a consistent format for how you structure your practices. That way your athletes will know what to expect from you, and they'll learn what you expect from them. This consistency in formatting will help practice to flow much easier. Table 9.4 shows a sample practice plan.

Coaching Tip

Prior to your first game, make sure your team can handle basic team offensive and defensive situations, such as where to throw the ball with runners on base. If your league or level of play allows bunting, prepare your team to be able to get an out at first base.

You should begin each practice with a team talk, which should address the nature of the day's practice and it's objectives. This talk should be no more than 5–10 minutes. Answer any questions your players may have and then start the warm-up.

Plan practice to incorporate both offensive and defensive components, for individuals and the team as a whole. Use a variety of drills and keep practice moving. Try to structure your activities so your athletes aren't standing around doing nothing. Players often tend to lose interest fast and will become a distraction for those athletes who are actively participating. Keep your instruction positive and put a little fun into your day!

At the conclusion of practice, you should plan a short team talk. Share with your players your general observations of whether your expectations were met at practice and what you'd like to see done

AVOIDING MENTAL BREAKDOWNS

Talk to your athletes about what it means to make progress and to improve. Physical mistakes are part of the game of softball. Throwing errors and fielding errors are going to happen, and that's okay as long as everyone is giving her best effort. You want to try to eliminate the mental mistakes, or at least avoid making the same ones over and over. Mental mistakes often result from a lack of mental focus or from not paying attention. Players who consistently throw to the wrong base or forget to cover a base are mentally breaking down. This could be the result of not paying attention or failure to preplan the play. Prior to each pitch, your athletes should be preplanning, or thinking about what they are going to do with the ball if it comes to them. That way they are ready to make the play when the ball is hit to them and there are no surprises!

Table 9.4   Sample Two-Hour Practice Plan

WHIZ KIDS
PRACTICE PLAN

DATE: June 16

AREAS OF FOCUS: Glove skills on individual defensive play, relays and cut-offs in the transition game, individual offensive skills

EQUIPMENT NEEDED: Bases, throwing balls, hitting balls, extra home plates, bats, 2 batting tees, tennis balls, protective screens

6:00 p.m.–6:10 p.m.: Team Talk

Talk about what the team has been doing well and what the team needs to improve upon in practice today. Be specific!

6:10 p.m.–6:20 p.m.: Warm-Up

Jog around field, stretch routine, blob tag game for sprints today

6:20 p.m.–6:30 p.m.: Individual Throwing and Catching Routine

Partner up and throw to loosen arms, gradually lengthen throws

Infielders: Partner up and do 10 short-hops each

   Do 10 forehands and 10 backhands each with partner rolls

Outfielders: Partner up and do 10 crow-hops to partner throwing in the air

   Do 10 crow-hops to partner with 1-hop throws

6:30 p.m.–6:40 p.m.: Individual Defensive Fielding Skills

Infielders: Take ground balls in 2 lines on infield dirt

Outfielders: Take grounders and flies in 1 line on outfield grass

6:40 p.m.–7:00 p.m.: Team Defense

Relays and cut-offs

Put nine defensive players on the field at a time and use the rest of the team as base runners. Rotate runners and fielders.

7:00 p.m.–7:45 p.m.: Individual Offense

Hitting stations. Divide the team into 4 groups of 4 players each and rotate around hitting stations when signaled by the coach.

Station #1: Hitting Practice–Coach throws batting practice with whiffle balls. Batter gets 8 strikes and teammates shag balls, then switch hitters.

Station #2: Bunting Practice–Coach tosses pitches to batter for sacrifice bunts, slaps. Batter must execute 4 successful bunts of each kind before switching. Teammates shag.

Station #3: 2 Batting Tees–One player hits balls into a screen while a partner tees up balls. Two tees operate simultaneously. Batter hits 10 balls then switches with partner.

Station #4: Soft toss with tennis balls. Coach tosses tennis balls to hitter while teammates shag. Hit 10 pitches then switch.

7:45 p.m.–7:55 p.m.: Warm Down

Easy throwing and light stretching

7:55 p.m.–8:00 p.m.: Team Talk

Announcements, if any

differently next time, if anything. Address the team's work ethic, execution that day, and any overall progress that was made. Make any announcements that are necessary for future practices, games, events, and so forth.

Once you begin to play games with opponents, your teams' weaknesses will be exposed. Don't get frustrated; this is part of the process. As you observe specific things your team needs to work on, jot them down in a notebook and use those notes to plan your next practice.

HOW TO CONDITION YOUR TEAM

Conditioning-only activities, which are targeted to enhance fitness levels of children, are not recommended for young athletes ages 13 and under. Instead, conditioning should occur as a result of practice activities designed to enhance skill development and learning that is specific to the sport of softball. You will find conditioning to be a by-product of many of the drills you will use at practice.

To enhance fitness levels in young players, include practice activities that involve the use of small groups and that keep players moving, requiring their continuous involvement in the activity. Circuit training is an excellent example of this type of conditioning and is a great way to teach batting. By dividing the team up into small groups and having them attend a sequence of stations, players can focus on specific elements of batting and get increased numbers of repetitions. Specific portions of the swing can be isolated, and teaching can be highly effective in smaller groups. Because of the smaller groups, all players are kept active and fitness levels can be enhanced or maintained.

Coaches should keep players hustling on the field between drills and activities and anytime athletes are moving on and off the field during games. Hustle works not only to enhance fitness levels in players, but also to keep athletes from becoming lethargic or lazy. A team that hustles on and off the field, whether at practice or in a ball game, looks sharp and sets a tone as a team that is intent upon its mission.

Weight training is a form of conditioning that enhances muscular strength or endurance. Weight training for strength gains is very specific in that strength gains are limited to the muscles being used and the degree to which the muscles are moved. For example, if a weight is placed in the hand and the arm is isolated so that the elbow only bends half way, then strength gains can be expected only in those muscles of the arm responsible for bending the elbow only in that specific range of motion.

Although weight training is not recommended for children, it may be safe for young athletes as young as 12 years of age, under certain conditions. For example, weight training may be considered safe if an adult who has been trained in lifting techniques for kids supervises the young athlete and if the youngster doesn't lift heavy weights. A heavy weight is any weight that the athlete has to strain to lift even once. Parents should be consulted before any attempt is made to engage young athletes in a weight training program.

HOW TO PREPARE FOR GAME DAY

No more dress rehearsals! Game day has finally arrived! No matter how well you prepare for this day, it can still be rather chaotic. Try not to sweat the little stuff, and don't worry about what you can't control. You'll have enough to think about on the day of the game.

The scope of your duties and responsibilities as coach may depend on how competitive your team is and the type of organization in which you are involved. For example, if umpires don't show up for your game, you may have to cancel it. If, however, you are involved in an organization that is highly sophisticated, you may be required to phone an assignor for replacement umpires who can be sent out within the hour. If you're the home team, you are responsible for umpires and field preparations.

You should be one of the first persons to arrive at the field on game day. Check the grounds to be sure that the field has been prepped properly (chalked correctly, bases available, correct distances set) and that the playing field is free of debris or hazardous conditions that may be unsafe for the participants. If bad weather is threatening, be sure you have a plan for taking appropriate action.

Make sure that all the necessary equipment arrives at the field before team warm-ups begin. If anything is missing at this point, you may still have time to make sure it gets to the field before the game begins. You should have the obvious team equipment needed to play the game on site: catcher's gear, throwing balls, hitting balls, bats, batting helmets, game balls, and the first-aid kit. As the coach, you will need rule book, line-up cards, score book, pens, pencils, important phone numbers, and tape for hanging the line-up card in the dug out. It's a good idea to keep all of your coaching necessities together in a zippered notebook or bag that is easy to grab on game day. Also, keep a small notepad handy to jot down game notes.

Once you have yourself situated and the playing field has been inspected, it's time to focus on the team. Take note of any players not present, which may effect your starting line-up. Check to see that all of your players are properly outfitted. There are specific rules pertaining to visors, hats, sleeves, and uniforms, so make sure you know the rules and explain them to the athletes prior to the game.

It is important to have a countdown of events leading up to game time. The countdown is a timed warm-up routine for your players that should be used prior to each and every ball game. It should be a logical order of events that the players follow on a consistent basis. A standard countdown may look something like this:

1:30–1:20	Light jog and stretch
1:20–0:50	Hitting drills
0:50–0:45	Sprints
0:45–0:35	Ball drills
0:35–0:30	Throwing routine
0:30–0:20	Infielders take grounders and outfielders take flies
0:20–0:12	Visiting team takes pre-game infield (home team coach gives pre-game talk)
0:12–0:04	Home team take pre-game infield (visiting team coach gives pre-game talk)
0:04–0:01	Coach's/umpire's meeting at home plate
0:00	Play ball!

Have a coach monitor the team's warm-up activities to give you time to write the line-up. The line-up card can be filled out in advance, as long as the players listed in the starting line-up are present at game time. Fill out the line-up card by listing the players in order of their appearance at the plate (batting order). In general, the batting positions in the line-up call for a certain strategy when determining the batting order. The underlying strategy is as follows:

Position in Line-Up	Type of Hitter
1	Good eye at the plate, excellent speed and base running ability, good contact hitter–someone with a high on-base percentage
2	Excellent bunter, good eye at the plate, good speed
3	Best hitter on team, rarely strikes out, great contact hitter
4	Second best hitter on team, is capable of hitting the long ball
5	Fairly good contact hitter, has good speed, smart base runner
6	Fair hitter
7	Fair hitter
8	Fair hitter
9	Second lead-off spot, has abilities of lead-off hitter but plays back-up role

Post the line-up in the dugout where everyone can see it. Make sure you list all substitutes on the line-up card. Read the batting order to the team before the game begins. This will eliminate a lot of confusion early on and will help your players prepare for the offensive part of the game.

Once the game gets underway, the fun begins. Make sure you remain cognizant of the goals and objectives you have set for the season or game. Do you want to make sure everyone plays in the game? Have you planned when you will make substitutions? Encourage the players to talk to one another on the field. They will be nervous at first, but talking with one another will help to calm them down. Be encouraging, and let the kids have fun. Relax, this isn't the World Series. The game is for the kids.

One of the more challenging aspects of coaching on game day has to do with controlling your emotions with regard to umpires. Umpires are human beings, and they have good days and bad days. You won't always agree with every official's call, and there will be times when you were in a

Coaching Tip

Have your team watch the opponent take pre-game infield. Observe which outfielders possess the strongest and weakest arms. That information may help you make an informed decision when your players are running the bases.

better position to see a play then the umpire who called it. However, remember that the umpire is doing the best job possible.

Have you ever umpired softball or officiated some sport? If you have, you'll be left with a real appreciation for what it's like to umpire a game. It's not easy. Most umpires are trying hard to do a good job, and they want to get it right. Believe me, they're not in it for the money! What is important is that you remain professional at all times when talking to or working with officials. Most umpires are very approach-

Coaching Tip

Just prior to game time, give your team final instructions—goals, inspiring thoughts, or "just go out there and have fun" words. Briefly remind everyone of the signals you'll be giving and let the team do a cheer if they'd like.

able and will talk with you about a call if you have a question. Your approach will mean everything. By being professional and showing respect for others, you'll be setting a good example for your athletes, who will be watching the situation as well.

If you feel there was a bad call or an umpire was out of position to make a good call, make sure you ask the nearest umpire for "time-out" before you walk onto the field. Approach the umpire who made the call and politely ask for clarification of the call. If you feel the umpire was out of position and couldn't see the play well, share your observations with the official and then ask him or her to please check with the other umpire for help on the play. You may find that saying "please" will help. You may find, on occasion, that after umpires confer on a play, the call will go the other way. If, however, the umpire tells you he or she saw the play and doesn't need any help, say thanks and just walk away.

During the game, note things you observe on the field that you want to discuss with the team later. You will no doubt observe breakdowns between players that you'll want to work on in your next practice, so write that down. You'll be addressing the team after the game, so make note of the good things you see too. Sure, you'll be critiquing their play, but give them a pat on the back as well.

Following the game, you'll want to meet with the team for a brief post-game talk. Have your players exhibit good sportsmanship

Coaching Tip

You may protest an umpire's call if you find that a rule wasn't applied properly (e.g., too many bases awarded on an overthrow). You may not protest a call if it was a judgment call (e.g., runner safe because of missed tag). See your rulebook.

by shaking the hands of the opponent at mid-field when the game is over and then meet your players on the outfield grass on your side of the field. Begin your talk by talking about things they did well that game. Acknowledge individual achievements that were significant. Identify the things that need work and talk to the team about the importance of working hard to make forward progress. Save any "coaching" or new instruction for your next practice. Add any announcements that you would like to make regarding future games or practices, and end your talk by telling your young athletes in what way you are proud of them. If your players want to do a cheer, be a part of it. Keep your game notes to plan your next practice.

10

CONCLUSION

IN PREPARING TO write this concluding chapter, I wondered about the final message I would leave with you. I wanted the message to be meaningful, thought provoking, and yet completely truthful. The message had to have meaning beyond having basic knowledge of the game and how to conduct games and practices. It had to make an indelible impression on your soul and be something that you could carry with you in your heart every time you assumed your role of coaching young people.

And then it occurred to me what that message should be, for I was reminded of it when my senior catcher, Patty, came by my office to talk about the upcoming season. We were discussing some academic matters as they related to our travel schedule, and I commended her on the outstanding score she had received on the writing proficiency exam (WPE), which she had taken earlier in the school year. The WPE is a writing skills assessment test that is given to all college students in the State of California prior to graduation from a four-year institution. At Sacramento State, our student-athletes are required to take and pass the WPE to receive their undergraduate degrees. Patty had not only passed the test, but had achieved the highest score of anybody on my softball team.

When I commended Patty on her score, I mentioned that she must have written eloquently on her exam and how wonderful it was to love writing so much. Patty's response to my statement both surprised and saddened me. She told me how she had loved to write when she was a little girl, and that she had especially loved to write stories. Then, one day in the second grade, Patty's teacher gave the class an assignment to write a story and turn it in for a grade. Patty took on the assignment with great eagerness and wrote an especially good story for which she was very proud. When she received her story back from the teacher, Patty was stunned to learn that she hadn't done very well. Her teacher had written that the story was too long and should have been only two pages in length. As a result, Patty lost a lot of points on her work and received a poor grade. Patty was hurt and found the experience especially painful because she believed she had written an especially good story. The teacher had never even acknowledged Patty's effort or the depths to which she had gone in putting the piece together. Although Patty kept that writing assignment, she told me that after that experience, she never really enjoyed writing anymore. In one brief moment of time, the action of a teacher had crushed the spirit of a child and had changed that child's life forever.

Now, as a senior at Sacramento State, Patty is studying to be a teacher and someday hopes to work with elementary school children. She will always remember her second grade teacher and the lesson learned that day in second grade. Because of her experience, Patty is cognizant of the impact that she will someday have upon young children, and she vows to be sensitive to the efforts and accomplishments of her students. I have known Patty to be a very bright and sensitive young lady, and I have no doubt that she will make a fine teacher.

And so it goes with coaching. You will find yourself working with very young and impressionable young girls who have joined your team to have fun, be with others, and learn new skills. You will be introducing them to a world of new ideas, new experiences, and unparalleled mental and emotional growth. What you do as a coach is likely to have a profound impact on their lives. It will be up to you to make sure that their participation in the sports experience you provide will be meaningful, positive, and productive in helping them to learn new things and to grow.

Coaching can be a wonderful experience. Be a positive role model for your players, and guide them in their physical, mental, emotional, and social development. You have an opportunity to be one of the most influential people your athletes will ever come in contact with, and if you really care about the kids you will be doing the right thing. Coaches leave legacies, so make sure the legacy you leave is one that will be remembered well. Good luck!

APPENDIX: ORGANIZATIONS

For more information on coaching girls in softball you may contact the following organizations:

Amateur Softball Association (ASA)
2801 NE 50th Street
Oklahoma City, OK 73111
www.softball.org

American Sport Education Program (ASEP)
P.O. Box 5076
Champaign, IL 61825
www.asep.com

The Institute for the Study of Youth Sports
Michigan State University
East Lansing, MI 48824
[Also the home of PACE (Program for Athletic Coaches' Education)]
http://ed-web3.educ.msu.edu/ysi/

National Alliance for Youth Sports (NAYS)
2050 Vista Parkway
West Palm Beach, FL 33411
www.nays.org

National Association for Girls and Women in Sports
1900 Association Drive
Reston, VA 22091
www.aahpherd.org

National Fastpitch Coaches Association (NFCA)
409 Vandiver Drive, Suite 5-202
Columbia, MO 65202
www.nfca.org

Positive Coaching Alliance (PCA)
Athletics Department
Stanford University
Stanford, CA 94305-6150
www.positivecoach.org

The Women's Sports Foundation
Eisenhower Park
East Meadow, NY 11554
www.womenssportsfoundation.org

GLOSSARY

Backhand play   Defensive stop or catch made on a ground ball on the throwing side of the fielder.

Backhand toss   Short throw used by a player to quickly deliver the ball to a teammate. Executed from the fielding position by rotating the throwing hand around to a position inside the ball in preparing to make the toss. The toss is led with a bent elbow while stepping toward the target with the same side foot and keeping the fingers stiff.

Backstop   Wall or fence behind the catcher that is part of the perimeter of the playing field. Used to contain play and keep the ball and all fielders in bounds. Also protects spectators from play on the field.

Ball   A pitch is declared a ball by the umpire when the pitcher uses a legal underhand motion to deliver the ball so that it passes the batter outside of the strike zone and the batter does not swing. (*See* Strike zone).

Batting tee   Stem made of hard rubber or plastic that holds the softball (much as a golf tee holds a golf ball) for the batter to practice hitting. Used by hitters of all ages to isolate ball movement so that hitting fundamentals can be mastered.

Bunt defense   Strategy used by the defensive team to field a bunted ball and make outs to stop the offensive team from advancing baserunners.

Bunt   Batting technique used to get the ball down on the ground, usually in the area in front of home plate.

Center fielder   Defensive player responsible for covering the territory in center field. (Center field is the area of the outfield that is directly behind second base when viewed from home plate.)

Change-up pitch   Pitch that travels toward home plate at a much slower speed than other pitches. Effective at fooling the batter into swinging too early.

Courtesy runners   Players who run for the pitcher and/or catcher after they bat. Allowed in youth ball only.

Crow-hop   Outfield technique used in the windup of a throw to help a player throw farther.

Cut-off player Player who is in the direct line with a throw from an outfielder to any base on the infield. Her job is to catch and stop a throw from an outfielder when it is either too late to get the runner out at the intended base and a play must be made on a trailing runner, or if the runner stops and doesn't advance to the next base.

Dead ball area (*See* Out-of-play area)

Defo Player who is listed in the line-up in the tenth spot and who plays defense only.

Designated player (DP) Player who is listed in the line-up as a batter only. The defensive player for whom the DP is batting is listed as the Defo and plays defense only.

Double play Defensive play that results in the elimination of two baserunners in rapid succession.

Drag bunt Offensive strategy in which the batter executes a quick bunt to surprise the defense to get on base.

Drop ball pitch Pitch that travels toward home plate with a downward trajectory. One of the easiest pitches to learn and throw. Used to get batters to hit ground balls, reducing the chance of long fly balls.

Drop step Quick step used by a player to move back on a ball hit over head.

Fair ball Batted ball that is directly hit into fair territory that either settles on the ground or is first touched while fair.

Fair territory Area of the field from home plate to the outfield fence between first base and third base into which batters try to hit the ball.

Fastball Pitch thrown at high speed with a straight trajectory.

First and third play Play in which there are runners on first and third bases respectively. The offense tries to get the defense to make a play on the runner advancing to second base so that the runner from third can score. The defense tries to put out the runner stealing second while keeping the runner at third from scoring.

Force out Out that occurs when a runner, who is being forced to advance to the next base because of a preceding runner, is either tagged with the ball while advancing or put out with the ball arriving at the base ahead of a runner in the possession of the defense.

Forehand play Defensive stop or catch made on a ground ball on the glove side of the fielder.

Foul ball Batted ball that is directly hit into foul territory or is first touched while foul.

Foul territory Area outside of the foul lines.

Hit and run Strategy used by the offensive team with a runner on base. The base runner leaves the base with the pitch and the batter hits the ball regardless of where it is pitched. If the ball is hit into a strategic location, it is possible for the runner to advance two bases on the hit if the play is well executed.

Hole Hitting lane between two defensive players on the field.

Infielders   Defensive players whose areas of responsibilities are on the infield, or the dirt area that encompasses the pitcher's mound, home plate, and all three bases.

Lead runner   Runner on base closest to getting to home plate.

Lead off   Movement of a base runner leaving a base when the ball is being pitched.

Left fielder   Defensive player responsible for covering the territory in left field. (Left field is the area of the outfield that is on the left when viewed from home plate.)

Outfielders   Defensive players whose areas of responsibility are in the outfield, or the grassy area beyond the infield.

Push bunt   Offensive technique of bunting the ball on the ground hard enough to get it past the incoming defensive fielder. Effective against a defense that is aggressively defending the bunt by playing close to home plate.

Relay   System of ball handling used by the defense when a long throw requires the use of a middle infielder to help get the ball to a base on the infield.

Right fielder   Player responsible for covering the territory in right field. (Right field is the area of the outfield that is on the right when viewed from home plate.)

Right-of-way rules   Establish who has priority when a ball is hit in the air to a portion of the field that has more than one person covering it.

Rise ball   Pitch that travels toward home plate with an upward trajectory. A difficult pitch to learn to throw, it must have good velocity in order to be effective.

Rundown   Situation in which a base runner is trapped off base between two defensive players.

Sacrifice bunt   Offensive technique of bunting the ball so that the defense has to make a put out on the batter at first base instead of the lead base runner.

Side arm throwing   Short, quick throw executed by an infielder from her fielding position. Player stays low in her fielding position and brings the throwing arm back below shoulder level to throw to the intended target.

Signals   (1) Combinations of numbers that the catcher uses to tell the pitcher to throw specific pitches. (2) Signs that players and coaches give to each other by touching different parts of their bodies or clothing, or some other action, that corresponds to a certain play or strategy.

Slap bunt   Offensive bunting technique used to draw the defense in toward home plate as if the batter were going to sacrifice bunt. At the last minute, the batter pulls the bat back and hits the ball on the ground into either infield alley.

Squeeze bunt   Offensive bunting technique used to surprise the defense and score a runner from third base. It is effective when the first and third basemen are playing back and are expecting the batter to swing away.

Steal   When a base runner legally vacates her base on the pitch and successfully gets to the next base before being tagged out and the ball is not hit by the batter.

Strike zone   Generally the area over the plate between the batter's shoulders and knees.

Strike   A pitch is declared a strike by the umpire when the pitcher uses a legal underhand motion to deliver the ball so that it passes through the batter's strike zone or when a pitch is swung on and is either missed or fouled off out of play.

Tag outs   (*See* Tag play)

Tag play   Out that occurs when a fielder with the ball securely in her hand or glove touches a runner who is off the bag.

Tracking   Ability of a player to visually follow a pitched or batted ball and anticipate where the ball will best be intercepted.

Transition game   How the infielders and outfielders work together to handle balls hit into the outfield when there are runners on base.

Underhand throwing   Short, quick throw used by an infielder to toss the ball to a teammate form her fielding position. From the fielding position, the infielder rotates her throwing hand to a position under the ball and uses a shoveling motion to toss the ball to a teammate.

REFERENCES

Amateur Softball Association (ASA) Rule Book, 2001, Oklahoma City.

Amateur Softball Association (ASA) Web Site, November 2000 (www.softball.org).

Amateur Softball Association (ASA) Web Site, January 2001 (www.softball.org).

American Sport Education Program. (1994). *SportParent*. Champaign, IL: Human Kinetics.

Borms, J. (1986). The child and exercise: an overview. *Journal of Sports Sciences*, 4, 3–20.

Carpenter, L. (1998, November/December). The United States Supreme Court and Sexual Harassment. Clarification of Issues. *Strategies*, 8–10, 18.

Coakley, Jay (1993). Social Dimensions of Intensive Training and Participation in Youth Sports. In *Intensive Participation in Youth Sports*, edited by B. Cahill & A. Pearl. Champaign, IL: Human Kinetics.

Gill, Diane L. (1995). Gender Issues: A Social-Educational Perspective. In *Sport Psychology Interventions,* edited by S. Murphy. Champaign, IL: Human Kinetics.

Golub, S. (1992). *Periods, From Menarche to Menopause*. London: Sage Publications.

Jaffee, L., & Sickler, H. (1998). Boys and girls choices of equipment and activities on the playground. *Melpomene Journal* 17(2), 18–23.

Martens, Rainer. (1990a). Risk Management. *Successful Coaching,* 169–193. Champaign, IL: Leisure Press.

Martens, Rainer. (1990b). *Successful Coaching*, Champaign, IL: Leisure Press.

Martens, R., Christina, R., Harvey, J., & Sharkey, B. (1981). *Coaching Young Athletes*. Champaign, IL: Human Kinetics.

Moffitt, T., Caspi, A., Silva, P., & Belsky, J. (1992). Childhood Experience and the Onset of Menarche: A Test of a Sociobiological Model. *Child Development* 63, 47–58.

NCAA News. "Opportunity Knocking" by Vanessa L. Abell. March 23, 1998.

1999–2000 High School Athletics Participation Survey, The National Federation of State High School Associations (NFSHSA), NFHS Web Site, November 2000 (www.nfhs.org).

Numminen, P., & Saakslahti, A. (1996, October). Gender differences—Are they dominant already in the early years? *AIESEP Newsletter* 53, 4.

Roberts, Wess. (1987). *Leadership Secrets of Attila the Hun.* New York: Warner Books.

Silby, C. (2000). *Games Girls Play.* New York: St. Martin's Press.

Smith N., Smith, R., & Smoll, F. (1983). *Kidsports: A survival guide for parents.* Reading, MA: Addison-Wesley.

Smith, Ronald E. (1998). A Positive Approach to Sport Performance Enhancement: Principles of Reinforcement and Performance Feedback. In *Applied Sport Psychology: Personal Growth to Peak Performance,* edited by Jean M. Williams. Mountain View, CA: Mayfield Publishing.

Sternberg Horn, T., Lox, C., & Labrador, F. (1998) The Self-Fulfilling Prophecy Theory: When Coaches' Expectations Become Reality. In *Applied Sport Psychology: Personal Growth to Peak Performance,* edited by Jean M. Williams. Mountain View, CA: Mayfield Publishing.

Strauss, S. (1992). *Sexual Harassment and Teens.* Minneapolis: Free Spirit Publishing.

Vogel, Paul. (1992). Planning for the Season. In *Youth Softball, A Complete Handbook,* edited by J. Elliot & M. Ewing. Carmel, IN: Cooper Publishing.

Weiss, M., & Chaumeton N. (1992). Motivational orientations in sport. In *Advances in sport psychology,* edited by T. S. Horn. Champaign, IL: Human Kinetics.

Weiss, M. R., Smith, A. L., & Theeboom, M. (1996). That's what friends are for: Children's and teenagers' perceptions of peer relationships in the sport domain. *Journal of Sport and Exercise Psychology* 18, 347–379.

The Women's Sports Foundation Education and Prevention Policy: Sexual Harassment and Unethical Relationships Between Coaches and Athletes. The Women's Sports Foundation Web Site, 1998 (www.womenssportsfoundation.org).

The Women's Sports Foundation Web Site, 1999 (www.womenssportsfoundation.org).

Youth Sports Institute. (1977). *Joint legislative study on youth sports program, phase II.* East Lansing, MI: Institute for the Study of Youth Sports.

INDEX

Accountability, 31
Adolescence, 39–40
Age, 25, 40, 101, 105
Amateur Softball Association (ASA), 4,
    61–62, 73, 74
American College of Sports Medicine, 48
American Psychiatric Association, 47–48
American Sport Education Program, 50
Anorexia, 47, 48
Arm circles, 111
Assistant coaches, 70–72, 135, 137, 147,
    183
Authority, 3, 6, 8, 36

Backhand toss, 88, 91
Backstop, 75
Balance, 125
Baserunning, 79, 132–142
    courtesy runners, 77
    drawing the throw, 132, 135–136
    drills, 132, 138–139
    home to first, 133–134
    leading off, 132, 136–137, 142
    momentum start sequence, 139
    overrunning first base, 134
    rounding a base, 134, 135
    rules of, 79
    scoring, 74
    slow runners, 145
    speed for, 132, 144
    tagging up on a fly ball, 137, 135–136
    tips for, 137

touching all bases, 135, 136
Bat, 60–62, 63
    anatomy of, 117
    ASA-approved, 61–62
    caring for, 63
    dropping, 126
    hitters and, 60
    holding, 117, 118
    length, 61
    weight, 60–61
Batting, 116–131. *See also* Bunting; Hitting
    bunting, 116
    follow-through, 122
    helmets, 13, 58, 62
    order, 77
    practice, 27
    rules for, 78
    stance, 116–118
    strike zone, 78, 101
    substituting batters, 77
    swing, 118–121
    technique, 115–116
    timing for, 109, 117
    tracking the ball, 121
Batting average, 116
Blocking for body angle, 114
Body language, 20, 21–22. *See also*
        Nonverbal communication
Boys
    coaching girls vs., 39
    psychological development, 39, 44–46
    reason for dropping sports, 32

Boys *(continued)*
  reason for playing sports, 39
  skills excelled at, 40
  social skills, 39
  societal expectations of, 45
  view of failure, 41–42
Broken bones, 17
Bruises, 16, 17
Bulimia, 47–48
Bumps, 16
Bunt and run strategy, 145
Bunt defense, 158–161
Bunting, 122–131, 145–146. *See also*
  Batting
  contact, 124–126
  drag bunt, 122, 128–131, 132
  in fast-pitch play, 73
  pivot, 123–124, 127
  "present the ball," 123
  push bunt, 126–127
  running into the ball, 126
  sacrifice bunt, 122–126
  slap bunt, 128, 129
  squeeze bunt, 127–128, 131, 143–144
  strategies for, 145–146
  tracking the ball, 125

Calendar checklist, 5
California Grapettes, 30
Captains, 22
Catcher
  cut-off calls by, 156
  gear, 13, 62, 114
  pitcher and, 81, 104
  position and coverage area, 65, 161
  receiving throws for force plays,
    113–114
  responsibilities (table), 68
  signals to pitcher, 104
  with weak arm, 146
Catching, 64–65, 89–93, 96, 114
  above the waist, 92
  backhand catch, 92
  below the waist, 92

  body position, 91, 93
  forehand catch, 92
  glove positions, 90–91, 92
  right-of-way rules, 64–66
  whole vs. part learning for, 27
Catching a pitch, 109–114
  blocking softball, 112–113
  down position, 110–111, 112
  giving signals, 112
  ready position, 110
  receiving throws for force plays,
    113–114
  receiving throws for tag plays, 113
  throwing out runners, 111–112
  up position, 111, 112
Catching the ball with the bat, 131
Center fielder
  position and coverage area, 65, 67
  responsibilities (table), 69
  right-of-way rules, 65, 67
Certification programs for coaches, 46
Change-up pitch, 109
Chest protectors, 13, 62
Choke up, 117
Clothing, 30
Coach, 1–18, 46
  assistant coaches, 70–72, 135, 137,
    147, 183
  certification programs for, 46
  game-day responsibilities, 182–186
  leadership qualities of, 2, 6–8
  liability of, 12–18
  positive vs. negative (table) techniques
    for, 3
  role of, 1–4
  style of, 3, 8, 9–12
  successful, 10–12
  time commitment, 4–6
Coaching tips
  avoid lazy catching, 93
  being decisive, 6
  coach's pep talk, 185
  communication between players, 20
  correcting mistakes, 21

dealing with problem parents, 51
decision making, 11, 26
encouraging outfielders to talk, 155
enhancing peer relationships, 45
expanding your knowledge, 2
giving praise, 10, 36
handling power, 7
observing opponents, 184
outfielder practice, 71
positioning fielders, 156
practicing skills, 177
prior to first game, 179
recording baserunning times, 144
reducing stress, 46
rewarding players, 37
rules and penalties, 31
sportsmanship, 27
success as self-improvement, 34
succes vs. winning, 172
support staff goals, 174
tracking the ball, 121
umpire's calls, 186
Commitment. *See* Time commitment
Communication, 20–26. *See also* Meetings;
    Signals
    age levels and, 25–26
    between players, 20
    miscommunications, 9, 21
    with parents, 22–24, 50, 176–177
    for positive relationships, 24
    verbal vs. nonverbal, 20, 21–22
Competence, 44–45
Competition, 46, 51–53
Conditioning activities, 3, 15, 40, 111,
    181–182
Confidence, 6–7
Consequences, 36–37
Consistency, 9, 10, 11, 30, 31, 183
Contact hitter, 145
Cool-down activities, 14, 16
Cooperation, 36
Courtesy runners, 77
Criticism, 3, 20, 21
Crossover step, 94–95, 97

Crow-hop throwing technique, 98
Cut-off players, 154–156, 157
Cuts, 16

Dead ball area, 74
Decision-making, 6, 7, 9, 10, 11, 26
Defense, 63–69, 74, 75, 77
    changing positions, 75–77
    defending a hole, 67
    numbers for positions, 67, 70
    responsibilities of, 66, 68–69
    right-of-way rules for, 67
    rules for, 74
    skills/abilities, 178
    starting positions, 64, 65, 67
    substituting players, 77
Defensive play, 81–114
    catching, 89–93, 96
    catching a pitch, 109–114
    fielding fly balls, 94, 97–100
    fielding ground balls, 93–97, 98,
        153
    pitching, 101–109
    practicing skills, 81–82
    throwing, 82–88, 89
Defensive strategies, 151–170
    basic situations, 152–154
    bunt defense, 158–161
    double play, 162–164
    first and third play, 168–170
    rundown, 165–168
    slap bunt defense, 161
    transition game, 154–158
Demonstrating new skills, 26
Designated player (DP), 77
Diet
    eating disorders, 47–49
    nutrition, 48
Directional bunting, 131
Discipline, 19, 29–31
Distance
    measuring, 74–75, 76, 77
    for pitching, 73, 77
Double play, 162–164

Double play defense, 162–164
    baseball vs. softball, 162
    initial throw, 162–163
    mindset needed, 162
    pivot, 163–164
Double steal, 146
Drag bunt, 128–131
Drawing the throw, 135–136
Drills
    baserunning, 138–139
    bunting, 131
    catching, 96, 114
    fielding ground balls, 102
    hitting, 124–125
    introducing new challenges with, 33
    offensive strategy, 148
    pitching, 110–111
    sliding, 27–29
    structured, 3, 33
    throwing, 90–91
Drop ball pitch, 105, 107
Dropping out, 32–33
Dropping the bat, 126
Drop step, 99–100
Drugs and alcohol, 30

Eating disorders, 47–49
Emergencies, 16–17. *See also* Injuries;
    Safety issues
Emotional control, 184–185
Emotional stamina, 6–8
Equipment, 58–63, 64
    bat, 58, 59, 60–62, 63
    batting helmet, 58, 62
    batting tee, 59
    cleats, 58, 59
    game day, 182–183
    gloves, 58, 59, 60
    masks, 13, 62, 114
    nets for batters, 59
    personal, 58, 59
    pitching machines, 14, 59, 63, 101
    for reducing risk of injury, 57
    safety of, 13, 16
    shoes, 59

softball, 58, 59, 62–63, 64
    throw-down bases, 58–59
Evaluation. *See* Feedback

Failure, 7–8, 34, 41–42, 52
Fair ball, 78
Fairness, 9, 10, 11, 30
Fair territory, 74
Fastball, 102, 103, 105
Fast-pitch, 73, 75, 77, 81, 101
Fear, 29, 52, 141, 142
Feedback, 12, 20, 21, 27
Female Athlete Triad, 48–49
Fielding fly balls, 94, 97–100
    blocking the sun and, 94
    dropping back, 99–100
    fielding position, 99
    playing the angle, 100
Fielding ground balls, 93–97, 98,
    102, 153
    backhand play, 96–97
    fielding position, 95
    forehand play, 96, 97
    getting to the ball, 94–95
    by infielders, 153
    by outfielders, 97, 98
    preparing to throw, 95
    ready position, 94
    strategies for, 153
Field of play, 14, 74–75, 76
Figure eight pitch, 101
First aid, 15, 16, 17. *See also* Injuries;
    Safety issues
First and third play, 146, 168–170
    defense, 168–170
First base, 133, 134, 135
First base coach, 135
First baseman
    body positioning for, 93
    as cut-off player, 156
    positions and coverage area, 65
    responsibilities, 63–64, 68
    right-of-way rules, 67
Fly balls
    fielding, 94, 97–100

tagging up on, 137, 135–136
Force out, 79, 152, 153
Force plays, 113–114, 152
Forehand toss, 87–88, 91
Foul balls, 78, 78
Foul territory, 74, 75, 76
Four-seam rotation (spin), 102–103, 105, 107
Fun
    during practice, 33, 179
    enthusiasm for coaching and, 11, 179
    as reason for playing, 3, 19–20, 31, 34, 44

Games, 72–79
    baserunning, 79
    batting, 78
    field of play, 14, 74–75, 76
    home vs. visiting, 73
    learning rules of, 58
    pitching, 58, 77–78
    players and substitutes, 75–77
    post-game talk, 185–186
    pre-game warm-up, 183
    preparation for, 182–186
    rules, 74
    scoring, 67, 74
Gear. *See* Equipment
Gender issues. *See* Boys; Girls
Girls
    coaching boys vs., 39
    concern with appearance, 45
    psychological development, 39, 44–46
    reason for dropping sports, 32
    reason for playing sports, 39
    skills excelled at, 40
    social skills, 39
    societal expectations of, 45
    view of failure, 41
Gloves, 60
    blocking sun with, 94
    fielder's, 59
    mitts, 60
    position for catching, 90–91, 92
Goals, 173–174
Grip
    for change-up pitching, 109

for drop ball, 105, 107
    fastball grip, 103
    pitching, 102–103, 105, 107, 108, 109
    rise ball pitching, 108
    sacrifice bunt, 123
    throwing grip, 82–83
Ground balls, fielding, 93–97, 98, 102, 153

Health concerns. *See also* First aid;
    Injuries; Safety issues
    eating disorders, 47–49
    hydration, 48
    medical information on players, 16, 17
Helmets, 13, 58, 62
Hip rotation and pivot, 124
History of softball, 72–73
Hit and run strategy, 145
Hitters, types of, 184
Hitting, 124–125. *See also* Batting
    adjusting to the pitch, 117, 119–120
    batting average for, 116
    practice, 115
    swing and, 118, 119–120
    timing for, 117
Hole, 67
Home plate, 75
Home runs, 115
Home team responsibilities, 178
Home team vs. visiting team, 73
Home to first, baserunning, 133–134, 138
Hydration, 48
Infield, 63, 64, 130, 133, 157
Infielders. *See also specific positions*
    body positioning, 91, 93, 159
    coverage areas, 63–64, 65, 66, 160
    defense strategies, 153–154
    grip on the ball, 83
    as relay players, 156–157
    responsibilities of, 64
    right-of-way rules, 65–66
    starting positions, 66, 154
Injuries, 13–18, 57. *See also* Safety issues
    common types, 16
    cool-down and, 14, 16

Injuries *(continued)*
    equipment and, 57
    from improper throwing, 84
    prevention and treatment, 14–18
    procedures for, 16, 17
    warm-ups and, 14
Innings, 73, 74
Insurance, liability, 13, 16

Knight, Bobby, 8
Knowledge, 2, 9, 19
"K" position, 104, 110

Language, inappropriate, 8, 55
Lawsuits, 17. *See also* Liability; Sexual
    harassment
Leadership skills, 2, 6–8
Leading off, 136–137, 139, 142
Lead runner, 152–153, 155
Left fielder, 65, 67, 69
Left-handed batter, 120, 122, 129–131, 132
Leg guards, 13, 62
Liability, 12–18
    checklist, 16
    environmental safety, 13–14
    equipment safety, 12
    game day, 182
    for injuries, 13–18
    insurance for, 13, 16
Line-up, 184
Listening, 9, 10, 12, 22, 50
Long balls, 158
Losing vs. failing, 34, 175
Loss of consciousness, 17
Manager, 70, 72
Masks, 13, 62, 114
Matching up players, 13–14
Medical information on players, 16, 17
Medical issues. *See* Emergencies; Injuries;
    Safety issues
Meetings
    with captains, 22
    for clearing miscommunications, 21, 22
    with parents, 23–24, 50, 176–177
    with support staff, 72

Menstruation, 47, 49
Miscommunications, 21–22
Mistakes, 21
    mental, avoiding, 179
Mitts, 60. *See also* Gloves
Motivation, 9, 19–20, 31–34, 44–45

National Alliance for Youth Sports (NAYS),
    50
National Operating Committee on
    Standards for Athletic Equipment
    (NOCSAE), 62
Negative coaching techniques (table), 3
Negative reinforcement, 10
Negligence, 12, 17
Nonverbal communication, 20, 21–22
Nose bleeds, 16
Numbness, 17
Nutrition, 48

Offensive play, 74, 77, 115–142
    baserunning, 132–142
    batting, 116–131
    bunting, 122–131
    rules for, 74
    sliding, 140–141, 142
Offensive strategies, 144–146, 148
    bunt and run, 145
    double steal, 146
    eight basic plays (table), 145–146
    first and third, 146
    hit and run, 145
    how to use, 143–146
    sacrifice bunt, 145
    safety squeeze, 146
    signs and signals, 147–149
    skills/abilities, 178
    squeeze bunt, 145
    steal, 144, 146
    strengths and weaknesses and, 144, 149
Olympic Games, 6
One-knee throws, 91
Osteoporosis, 48
Outfield, defined, 63
Outfielders, 63

crow-hop throwing, 98
fielding ground balls, 97, 98
grip on the ball, 83
right-of-way rules, 65
transition game, 154–158
Outfield fence, 75
Out-of-play area, 74, 75
Outs, 74
force outs, 79, 152, 153
hand signals and, 147
lead runner and, 152–153
tag outs, 79
tag play, 152
Overhand throwing, 40, 82, 83–86
Overrunning first base, 134

Pain, sharp, 17
Parents
behavioral guidelines for, 24, 50
behavior problems with, 49, 51
communicating with, 22–24
education for, 46, 50
meeting with, 5, 23–24, 176–177
over-involvement of, 49, 50
problem parents, 7, 50, 51
rules, 174
setting goals for, 172
types of, 23
"Part" learning method, 28–29, 142
Peer groups, 7, 45
Peer pressure, 7, 50
Penalties, 30–31
Performance goals, 17, 175
performance goal plan, 176
Personal skills. See Social skills
Physical contact. See also Sexual harassment
appropriate vs. inappropriate, 54–55
Pitcher
catcher and, 81
as cut-off players, 156
gear, 58
position and coverage area, 65
responsibilities of, 68
right-of-way rules, 66
wild, 145

Pitching, 71, 101–109, 110–111
age for, 101, 105
basics, 101–102
change-up, 109
coaches for, 71
delivery styles, 101
distance, 73, 74–75, 76, 77
drop ball, 105, 107
fast-pitch, 73, 75, 77, 81, 101
follow-through, 105
grip, 102–103, 107, 108, 109
knowledge of, 71
private instruction, 101
rise ball, 107–108
rules, 77–78
slingshot pitch, 101
stance, 104
the pitch, 104–105
warming up, 58
Pitching machines, 14, 59, 63, 101
Planning for practice, 177–181
sample practice plan, 180
Planning for the season, 171–186
overview, 171–172
setting goals, 172–176
Play calling (signals), 104, 112, 143, 147–149
Players
designated player (DP), 77
matching up, 13–14
number of, 74, 75
playing favorites, 11
setting goals for, 172
starting player, 77
substituting, 75–77
Playing favorites, 11
Playing field, 14, 74–75, 76
Position play, 62–69. See also individual positions
for defensive positions, 64, 65, 66
right-of-way rules, 64–66
Positive coaching techniques (table), 3
Positive role models, 35–36
Practice, 177
Practice stations, multiple, 27

Praise
  balancing criticism with, 21
  constructive feedback and, 27
  during instruction, 41
  by players, 10
  for social skills, 36
Psychological development, 39, 44–46
Push bunt, 126–127

Quick-snap throwing, 82, 86, 90
Quitting, reasons for, 3, 5, 32–33

Raybestos Brakettes, 6
Raymond, Ralph, 6
Relay, 156–159
  body position, 159
  infielders as relay players, 156–157
  positions for long balls, 158
  second baseman as relay player, 157, 158
  shortstop as relay player, 157, 158
Respect
  for authority, 3, 6, 36
  between coach and player, 54
  discipline and, 19
  for rules, 7, 31
  teaching, 11, 12
Rewards, 34, 37
Right fielder, 65, 67, 69
Right-handed batting, 120, 129, 130
Right-of-way rules, 64–66, 67
Rise ball pitch, 107–108
Risk, managing, 17
Rober, Louis, 73
Role models, 35–37
  assistant coaches as, 71
  coaches as, 2, 9, 35
  integrity and, 11–12
  positive traits for, 9, 35–36
Rules, 29–31, 74
  of ASA, 74
  for drugs and alcohol, 30
  enforcing, 31
  fairness and, 30
  of the game, 58, 74
  for parents, 24, 50

penalties for breaking, 30–31
  player input for, 31
  of right-of-way, 64–66, 67
  spectator conduct guidelines, 50
  writing down, 29–30, 31
Rundown defense strategy, 165–168
Running bases. *See* Baserunning

Sacrifice bunt, 122–126, 145
  conditions for, 145
  contact, 124–126
  down first baseline, 126
  down third baseline, 126
  follow-through, 126
  hand grip, 123
  as offensive team strategy, 145
  pivot, 123–124, 127
  surprise element in, 127
  walking and, 123
Safety issues. *See also* Emergencies;
    Health concerns; Injuries;
    Liability
  for conditioning, 15, 181
  for environmental safety, 13–14
  first aid, 15, 16, 17
  game day, 182
  managing risk, 17
  matching up players, 12–14
  for pitching machines, 14, 59
  for playing fields, 14
  for using equipment, 12, 13, 14, 16
Safety squeeze, 146
Scare tactics, 10
Scorekeeper, 70, 72
Scoring, 67, 74, 78
Second baseman
  double play pivot, 164, 165
  position and coverage area, 65, 161
  as relay player, 157, 158
  responsibilities (table), 68
  right-of-way rules, 67
Self-esteem, 3, 20, 47, 48, 52
Self-improvement, 34, 45
Sexual harassment, 53–56
  appropriate physical contact vs., 54–55

avoiding potential problems, 54
language as, 55
trust and, 56
vulnerability of players and, 53–54
Short-handed rule, 75
Shortstop
double play pivot, 163–164
position and coverage area, 65, 161
as relay player, 157, 158
responsibilities, 69, 81
right-of-way rules for, 66, 67
"Show" pitch, 107
Shuffle (side steps), 94
Side-arm throwing, 82, 87
Signals, 104, 112, 143, 147–149
Size, matching up players, 13–14
Skills. *See also individual skills*
demonstrating, 26
girls vs. boys, 40
levels of, 25
teaching correctly, 13, 24
team play and, 149
whole vs. part learning of, 27
Slap bunt, 128, 129, 130
defense, 161
Sliding, 140–141, 142
body position, 28, 140, 141
fear of, 29, 141, 142
headfirst, 142
hook slides, 142
pop-up slide, 141, 142
practice, 27–29, 142, 140–141
Slingshot pitch, 101
Slow-pitch, 73
Snap throw, 166
Social development. *See* Social skills
Social skills. *See also* Respect
cooperation, 36
girls vs. boys, 39
honesty, 11
integrity, 11–12
learning through sports, 31, 41
positive role models and, 36
sportsmanship, 27, 36, 50
teaching, 1, 9, 36, 41

Softball basics, 178
Softball (balls). *See also* Grip
choosing, 58, 59, 62–63, 64
dropping, 166
optic yellow, 62, 64
for pitching machines, 59, 63
rotation (spin), 102–103, 105, 107, 108
Soto, Phil, 4
Spectator conduct guidelines, 50
Speed, for baserunning, 133, 144
Spin (ball rotation), 102–103, 105, 107, 108
SportParent, 50
Sportsmanship, 27, 36, 50
Sprains, 16
Squeeze bunt, 127–128, 131, 143–144, 145
"Squish the bug," 120
Staff. *See* Support staff
Starting player, 77
Stealing, 73, 146
Stress, 46, 51–53
Stretching, 14–15, 16
Strikes, 77–78, 101
Strike zone, 78, 101, 107
Substituting players, 75–77
Success
at coaching, 10–12
learning new skills as, 26
as motivation for playing, 32
practicing and, 82
as process vs. outcome, 33, 172
self-improvement as, 34, 45
structured learning and, 25
winning, 10, 17, 32, 33, 74, 172
Sun hazard, 94
Support staff, 58, 70–72
assistant coach, 70–72, 135, 137, 147, 183
choosing, 58, 70–72
handling disagreements, 71, 72
manager, 70
meetings with, 72
need for female coach, 70–71
rules, 174
setting goals for, 172

Swing, 118–121
  downswing, 118, 119
  hip rotation, 120
  hitting and, 118, 119–120
  launch position, 120
  pivoting, 120
  sequence for, 119–120
  shoulder rotation, 120–121
  stride for, 119–120
  tracking the ball during, 121

Tagging, 113, 166
Tag outs, 79
Tag plays, 152
Tardiness, 30
Teaching, 24–28
  based on age levels, 25–26
  based on skill levels, 28
  coaching as, 1
  communication skills for, 19
  techniques for, 19–20, 24–25, 26
  videotaping, 27
  whole vs. part, 27
Team
  defense, 178
  evaluations, 175
  goals, 174
  offense, 178
Tee ball, 101
10-and-under California Breeze, 4
Third base coach, 135, 137, 147
Third baseman
  as cut-off player, 156
  position and coverage area, 65, 161
  responsibilities (table), 69
  right-of-way rules, 67
Throwing, 82–88, 89, 90–91
  age and, 40

backhand toss, 88, 89, 91
  double play initial throw, 162–163
  forehand toss, 87–88, 91
  grip, 82–83
  "like a girl," 40
  overhand, 40, 82, 83–86
  quick-snap, 82, 86, 90
  side-arm, 82, 87
  snap throw, 166
  underhand, 82, 87–88
Time commitment, 4–5
Time-out, 185
Tracking the ball, 121, 125
Transition game, 154–158
Travel, 4, 30
Trust, 6, 7, 11, 53–54, 56

Umpire, 78, 185
  judgment calls, 185, 186
  protesting calls, 185, 186
Underhand throwing, 82, 87–88
United States Pan American softball team,
  8

Videotaping, 27
Visitors, 30, 50, 73

Walking, 123
Walking lead, 137, 142
Warm-up activities, 14–15, 183
Weight
  concerns about, 48
  eating disorders, 47–49
Weight training, 181–182
Windmill pitch, 101, 102, 104–105, 106
Windup, 83–84
Winning, 10, 32, 33, 74, 172
Women's Sports Foundation, 53

ABOUT THE AUTHOR

A native of Lansing, Michigan, Kathy Strahan holds a master's degree in physical education from Michigan State University. While a student-athlete at MSU, Strahan helped the Spartans to an AIAW National Championship in 1976 and the Big Ten Championship in 1978. An ASA All-American shortstop for the Raybestos Brakettes of Stratford, Connecticut, Strahan helped lead her team to National Championships in 1977, 1978, and 1980. She was also a member of the United States World Championship team in 1978 and a member of the gold medal United States Pan American team in 1979.

An eighteen-year veteran coach of major college softball, Strahan received Big West Conference Co-Coach-of-the-Year honors in 1989 and Western Athletic Conference (WAC) Coach-of-the-Year honors in 1993. She was inducted into the Michigan ASA Hall of Fame in January 1995 and will be inducted into the Greater Lansing Area Sports Hall of Fame in July 2001. She recorded her 500th career win in March 2001. She is currently the Head Softball Coach at California State University, Sacramento, and resides in Folsom, California.